COMBAT
TRACKING
GUIDE

COMBAT
TRACKING
GUIDE

John Hurth

STACKPOLE
BOOKS

Published by
STACKPOLE BOOKS
5067 Ritter Road
Mechanicsburg, PA 17055
www.stackpolebooks.com

Printed in the United States of America

First edition

Library of Congress Cataloging-in-Publication Data

Hurth, John.
    Combat tracking guide / John Hurth. — 1st ed.
        p.   cm.
    Includes index.
    ISBN 978-0-8117-1099-2
    1. Scouting (Reconnaissance) 2. Tracking and trailing. I. Title.
    U220.H87 2012
    355.4'13—dc23
                                                            2012005460

*This book is dedicated to all combat trackers,
past and present, as well as the men and women in uniform
who have served and continue to serve our great nation.*

Contents

Troops in Contact

"Certainly there is no hunting like the hunting of man
and those who have hunted armed men long enough and
liked it, never really care for anything else thereafter."
                                                    —Ernest Hemingway

Somewhere in the current theater of operations a small convoy of military vehicles winds its way down a narrow, unimproved road. The surrounding terrain is steep and rugged, and channelizes traffic. On the south side, the road butts up to a mountain, and from the north edge of the road, the terrain drops down into a cultivated area that eventually runs into an intermittent stream. On the north side of the stream the terrain gradually rises above the valley floor.

Approximately two hundred meters north of the stream, an enemy force is watching. Patiently, they wait for the lead vehicle to reach a culvert below the road surface. The culvert marks and conceals the location of an improvised explosive device (IED). As the lead vehicle in the convoy creeps over the culvert, the enemy initiates the ambush with the IED. There is a violent explosion and the vehicle is engulfed by a plume of smoke and dust. The force of the blast picks up the vehicle's front end and slams it back down to earth. The lead vehicle comes to an abrupt stop. As the smoke and dust begin to settle, the rear door on the passenger side opens and a soldier falls out. In shock and confusion, he tries to crawl to safety. The convoy stops behind the lead vehicle, which is now blocking the narrow road.

Immediately, the enemy opens fire from an elevated position across the stream with rocket-propelled grenades (RPGs) and small arms. Stunned by the sight of the lead vehicle's destruction, the soldiers scramble to reorient their weapons on the enemy and return fire. The chaos of battle ensues. The infantry platoon leader radios "troops in contact!" to the company tactical operations center. After assessing the enemy situation, the platoon leader requests assistance from the quick reaction force (QRF), along with immediate close air support.

The battle between the platoon and the ambushers carries on for almost thirty minutes. Just as abruptly as the fight began, however, it seems to end. The explosions of RPGs cease and the chatter of small-arms fire fades, and it appears to the soldiers on the ground that the enemy is breaking contact and retrograding from its fighting position.

Instantly, the platoon leader starts receiving ACE (ammo, casualties, and equipment) reports from his squad leaders, who inform him of four friendlies killed in action, three friendlies wounded, and one friendly vehicle destroyed. The squad leaders issue orders to their team leaders, who begin consolidating, reorganizing, and adjusting their perimeter. The platoon sergeant designates the casualty collection point while the platoon medic and combat life-savers feverishly attempt to save the lives of their wounded comrades. Minutes later, two A-10 Thunderbolts arrive on station and loiter overhead. The platoon leader has his joint terminal attack controller check in and coordinate with the aircraft to strafe the enemy's last known position.

The aircraft bank away and conduct a gun run, peppering the side of the mountain with 30 mm cannon fire. The aircraft pull up and off the target and continue to loiter overhead to give the platoon cover and time to prepare the convoy for movement out of the kill zone.

The platoon leader requests a medical evacuation and is told that it will take approximately forty minutes to arrive. The remaining soldiers—now low on ammo—quickly strip the destroyed vehicle of all remaining munitions and sensitive items. When they are done, they push it off the road. A squad leader moves down to the vehicle and throws two incendiary grenades into the vehicle to ensure it is totally destroyed before abandoning it.

The platoon begins cross-loading the remaining vehicles with the dead and wounded soldiers. Once they're finished, the platoon leader and platoon sergeant receive an "up" from the squad leaders that everyone is ready to move. The convoy slowly limps its way east two kilometers to a suitable helicopter landing zone to link up with the QRF and evacuate their dead and wounded.

One of the many difficulties military units face when conducting operations is locating and maintaining contact with a light, mobile, and elusive enemy. Too often the above scenario is the norm rather than the exception—a small enemy force strikes, contact ensues then breaks, and the attackers drift away without pursuit.

There is a military tactic that when properly employed will radically alter the scenario described and could thereby greatly change the outcome of the conflicts our forces fight. It is the use of *visual tracking techniques*—the efficient and aggressive pursuit of a footborne enemy by trained members of a combat tracking unit.

Unfortunately, visual tracking is perhaps the single most misunderstood, underused, and underestimated combat capability. Most of these erroneous opinions about visual tracking are based on misconceptions and misrepresentations that come from the tracking community. Trackers who teach holistic forms of tracking that focus their instruction on a spiritual aspect, or who teach programs that are technically and tactically unsound, have crushed any true debate on the virtues of tracking as a military specialty skill.

What most people do not understand is that it is virtually impossible for even a single person to move across any terrain for any distance without leaving some type of evidence of his passage. If one looks at sign left by the quarry and puts it into the context of military intelligence, then the physical evidence becomes intelligence indicators. And indicators observed by a trained tracker will provide immediate, valuable intelligence about the enemy: size of force, direction and rate of movement, infiltration and exfiltration routes as well as methods used, safe areas used, size of load and type of weapon being carried, age and sex, physical disabilities, state of training and discipline, and capabilities and intentions.

In an environment where information about an enemy is limited, the primary means of intelligence gathering will be through conducting dismounted patrols. The conduct of combat tracking operations closely mirrors the F3EAD targeting methodology:

Find the enemy force by identifying and following the forensic indicators it leaves behind. Following the enemy's tracks and analyzing the indicators left behind paints a picture of the enemy being pursued. The information gained from evaluating the enemy's track line reveals the enemy's pattern of life, which may include overnight locations, daily routes, villages visited, and likely support networks. Questioning potential witnesses along the way may also provide an opportunity to confirm or deny what the tracker is interpreting from the ground.

Fix the enemy and its location at the end of the track.

Finish: Tracking provides the opportunity for the finishing force to engage the enemy after the combat trackers have located its position. The force will normally not have time to create a detailed plan. Instead, it will need to adapt battle drills to the existing conditions and rapidly execute required actions: hasty attack, raid, ambush, or cordon and search. The patrol must also be prepared to conduct follow-on pursuit operations based on time-sensitive information found during the exploitation of the objective.

Exploit the objective once secured to gather information about the enemy, which feeds the intelligence operations cycle and leads to operations that yield more intelligence, leading to more operations.

Analyze enemy information quickly so if information is time sensitive it can be acted on immediately (an example would be information about another enemy location).

Disseminate all information gathered to everyone on the ground as well as to the higher command.

A combat tracking operation, like the targeting process, is continuous. At any given time, the combat tracker unit may be in any of the F3EAD targeting phases. One moment it may be in the Find phase only to quickly transition to the Exploit phase, followed by the appropriate Fix, Finish, Analyze, or Disseminate phases. The combat tracking operation is a fluid operation that takes the pursuers to wherever the evidence leads.

Historically, combat trackers have been used by many military and paramilitary units around the world with a great deal of success. The ability to employ combat trackers to pursue an enemy and regain contact, gather information, or find missing friendly personnel has proved to be a game-changing asset in numerous conflicts.

Should the situation present itself, every unit needs to be self-reliant and have the capacity to conduct exploitation and pursuit operations against the enemy without being dependent on outside resources, such as tracking dogs, unmanned aerial vehicles, or ground sensors. Obviously, these resources have their value, but the fact is that they are not always available. Furthermore, they are not always tactically appropriate. Indeed, history and careful analysis favor the visual tracker in terms of flexibility, cost efficiency, and overall mission success.

Combat tracking operations provide that sought-after "soldier sensor," who collects and reports information and is highly trained in the fundamental skill of observation. Virtually by definition, soldiers who are trained visual trackers have greater attention to detail and better situational awareness in any environment and on any mission. Through their training, they are ingrained with the habits of constant analysis, anticipation of diverse threats, and vigilance, and are able to detect, note, and report information of potential intelligence value.

THE ALTERNATIVE

Considering the potential effectiveness of the combat tracker unit employed on a tracking operation, let's return to our opening scenario, with a slight modification: After the explosion, contact, and A-10 gun run, the ambushed convoy consolidates and reorganizes. Explosive ordinance disposal (EOD) teams and weapons intelligence teams (WITs) are called in to exploit the incident site and conduct a handoff to a combat tracker squad, who initiates a pursuit operation against the elusive enemy.

When properly understood at the command and control levels, and when implemented by a well-trained combat tracker squad, the pursuit operation would look very much like the following.

An EOD team, WIT, and combat tracker squad all arrive at the outer cordon of the IED incident site. Once the IED location is identified, the EOD team quickly clears the area to ensure there are no secondary devices. Immediately the WIT and combat tracker squad (consisting of two four-man combat tracker teams) begin conducting coordinations. Once EOD notifies the WIT team leader that the area is safe, the WIT, minus two members, heads down to the blast seat to begin site exploitation. At the same time, the remaining two WIT members conduct a sweep around the outside of the incident site.

During the exploitation, a command wire is found heading north. A member of the WIT who has been trained in tracking is told where the command wire is so he can investigate and identify whether there is any evidence beyond the blast seat. Through initial investigation, the WIT tracker identifies two thin, enamel-covered copper wires draped over some tall grass. Looking further ahead, the WIT tracker attempts to identify where the wires go. He cautiously probes forward while everyone else remains behind to avoid contaminating the site. Within fifty meters of the detonation site, a cell phone used to initiate the IED is found in a small irrigation ditch. Observed on the other side of the ditch is the outline of a partial foot impression. The partial impression is clearly identified to be a military-style boot with a star-and-lug-type Vibram pattern.

Concurrently, the other two WIT members conducting their sweep detect what they believe to be the ambushers' entry and exit point at the stream's edge. Three sets of prints indicate a northerly direction of travel. One of the tracks is identified as the same military-style boot found in the ditch. The WIT members mark and record the suspected entry and exit point and continue to conduct their sweep.

After the two members of the WIT conclude their sweep, they report their findings to the WIT team leader and the combat tracker squad leader. The remaining WIT members continue to exploit the incident site, while the two WIT members who conducted the sweep guide the combat tracker squad, along with an infantry platoon in support, to the location of the enemy's entry and exit point.

The patrol stops short of the location while the WIT members, combat tracker squad leader, his lead tracker, and the tracker team leader all move up and assess the entry and exit point. The WIT members conduct a handoff with the combat tracker squad (call sign SIERRA-1). The combat tracker squad gathers as much information as possible from the footprint impression evidence associated with their quarry. The tracker determines they are tracking at least three men who were moving at a leisurely pace and that the foot impressions are no more than twelve hours old.

The squad leader returns and briefs the rest of the SIERRA-1 element. He also informs the platoon leader from the tracker support group of all information taken from the initial start point. As the lead tracker for the SIERRA-1 element follows the ambushers' sign, he interprets the track line in an attempt to get into the mind of the quarry. He observes that the stride patterns from the ambushers going toward the incident site are shorter than those going away and so concludes that they may have traveled during the night to place the IED and traveled back up the same route just about dawn.

As the SIERRA-1 tracker squad pursues the enemy, the rest of the platoon follows at a distance, so as to not give away the tracker squad's position, but close enough to deploy quickly if the trackers make contact. When the squad reaches the top of a hill overlooking the incident site, they discover the ambush position. The squad leader halts the patrol to investigate the area with his alpha team leader and lead tracker. The rest of the squad provides security.

As the leaders investigate the ambush position, they discover twelve fighting positions. Evidence found at the site indicates the ambushers were armed with at least two RPG-7s (they see RPG-7 booster wrappers and damage caused by the back blast), two RPK machine guns (bipod leg impressions, 7.62x54R shell casings, and one 25-round non-disintegrating linked belt dropped by the fleeing gunner), and eight AK-47 rifles (7.62x39mm shell casings at each position with magazine impressions in the ground). A blood trail from one of the firing positions indicates that at least one attacker is wounded. The blood pool suggests the wound is in the left shoulder area.

While examining the foot impressions, the trackers notice that all of them except one were made by flat tennis-shoe soles with either a zigzag or diamond tread patterns. The one impression that stands out is a star and lug-type Vibram boot sole pattern with a definitive heel. This Vibram-type impression seems to move between the two RPG positions. The trackers conclude that the insurgent who wore the Vibram boots was either a foreign fighter or leader of the enemy element. They also discover the ambushers' track line departing from the ambush position in an easterly direction.

The squad leader quickly disseminates all information to his squad as well as to the platoon leader. The lead tracker team continues to follow the track line until it reaches a contaminated area of ground. The tracker halts before entering the contaminated area. As the lead tracker and team leader contemplate the scene, they realize that the ambushers must have stopped and rested.

The tracker moves cautiously around the scene, being careful not to contaminate the area further. He discovers a clump of discarded material soaked in blood. The material is still wet but some of the blood that leaked onto the ground is dry. It appears the injured attacker is bleeding profusely and will most likely slow his comrades down. The tracker, along with his team leader, counts the flattened and marred areas and determines that they are still following all twelve insurgents.

The lead tracker and team leader move around the rest area and detect two exit points leading in different directions. They determine that one enemy element consisting of eight people (including the individual with the Vibram sole) appears to still be moving east. Another group of four, including the wounded attacker, has shifted north.

The squad leader conducts a quick map reconnaissance of the area to figure out where each element may be heading. A village just north of the squads position is identified. Further scrutiny indicates that it would be the most logical destination for the ambushers with a wounded individual. The other element appears to be heading to a village near the border. The SIERRA-1 leader calls back to the platoon to inform the platoon leader of the details concerning the quarry's separation point. It is decided that SIERRA-1 will mark the quarry's separation point with orange surveyor tape upon which is written the time, date, and grid coordinates. This will help another tracker pursuit group identify the point later.

Meanwhile, the SIERRA-1 element continues to track the other eight ambushers. The platoon leader radios the company command post to alert the company commander as to the current situation. Immediately, another combat tracker squad (call sign SIERRA-3) with a platoon tasked as the tracker support group is notified to move to the separation point, and continue to follow the track line north. The company commander also contacts the battalion to request that a blocking force be deployed to keep the ambushers from reaching the village, or crossing the border. The SIERRA-3 tracker squad locates the surveyor's tape identifying the quarry's separation point and follows the quarry with the wounded insurgent, who traveled north to the village.

As the SIERRA-3 trackers near the village, they conduct a halt and provide surveillance on the target until the rest of the tracker support group can link up. Overwatch security is established, and the platoon enters the village. It discovers preparations for a funeral. Further investigation reveals that the wounded attacker bled out and died. The three remaining ambushers are discovered hiding among the villagers and apprehended thanks to the footprint evidence collected along the patrol. SIERRA-3 and the platoon complete their assigned mission and are extracted back to the forward operating base (FOB) for debriefing.

Almost simultaneously, SIERRA-1 aggressively follows its quarry to a shepherd's cabin west of the target village on the border. Blocking forces move into the village and provide a presence under the pretext of conducting a "village assessment." The SIERRA-1 trackers locate the ambushers and conduct surveillance on the target building until link up with the rest of the platoon occurs. Security is established to seal off the objective. Through the platoon's interpreter, a call-out is conducted. The ambushers open fire, and the platoon returns it in force. Seven attackers are killed during the firefight; three are wounded and immediately captured. The platoon and the SIERRA-1 trackers are directed to move to a helicopter landing site where aviation will pick up SIERRA-1 and the supporting platoon, as well as the wounded enemy, and transport them back to the FOB.

Upon returning to base, the combat tracker squads as well as the leaders of each platoon conduct a hot debrief performed by the company intelligence support team. The purpose of this is to collect time-sensitive information that may affect ongoing or future operations.

The combat trackers and platoons are then given twenty-four hours to stand down and produce a formal debrief report outlining the details of the mission. This will provide information collected and lessons learned. The report is entered into a database such as the Combined Information Data Network Exchange (CIDNE) to make all details of the mission available through query to intelligence analysts using Distributed Common Ground Systems (DCGS). This information can then be analyzed to produce intelligence products useful to commanders of future operations.

The differences between the military unit with visual tracker capability and the one without are evident in these two scenarios. Time and time again, military forces are opting for more expensive, less effective, and ultimately unsustainable forms of pursuit. But the IED has changed low-intensity conflict: highly advanced and enormously expensive technical solutions have proved over more than a decade to be ineffective. But, tucked in among the folds of American military history, lies the solution: a low-tech, low-cost, and time-tested skill inherent in the makeup of humans.

ABOUT THIS BOOK

Other combat tracking books provide little more than a hint of the possibilities and potential for combat tracking operations in hostile environments. This book seeks to provide the definitive manual of tracking techniques and operational methodology. You will find in these pages everything you need to know in order to understand modern combat tracking techniques and operational procedure. You will also find everything necessary to integrate and use this incredible force-multiplying capability to its best advantage.

1

Basic Visual Tracking

"As long as the criminal remains upon two legs so long must there be some indentation, some abrasion, some trifling displacement which can be detected."
—*Sherlock Holmes in "The Adventure of Black Peter," by Arthur Conan Doyle*

Edmond Locard was a pioneer in forensic science and director of the first crime lab in France at the beginning of the twentieth century. Locard introduced the basic principle in forensic science now known as Locard's exchange principle. He believed that no matter where you go or what you do, you leave some trace of evidence behind and take some trace of evidence from your environment with you. Locard's principle is a key concept a tracker must keep in mind if he is to catch his quarry. The tracker must realize that wherever his quarry goes and whatever his quarry does, he will leave behind some trace of himself, and take something along with him.

There are many ways to track humans. Generally, the two most common non-technical methods are scent tracking and visual tracking. Scent tracking is usually associated with the use of tracking canines, which are trained to track their quarry by using their keen sense of smell.

Visual tracking is typically associated with the human tracker, who tracks primarily by sight. The trained tracker *identifies, interprets,* and *follows* disturbances detected within the natural

1

environment. These disturbances can be in the form of impressions left on the ground, altered vegetation, litter discarded by the quarry, and many, many others. (Of course, human trackers also have the ability to use other senses to detect their quarry, especially hearing and smell.)

An individual who is trained to track has the ability to:

- Detect and identify the correct sign by the regularity and size of the impression, flattening of a surface, color change of the medium the quarry passed through in contrast to its surroundings, transfer of one medium onto another, amount of disturbance made within an environment, or litter discarded that may be associated with the quarry.
- Follow the track line and reacquire the track if it should be lost.
- Interpret the sign and track picture, the most important capability of the tracker. Anyone can learn how to track by following sign. A first-rate tracker, however, has the ability to interpret what he sees and form a picture of what the quarry did, is doing, or might attempt to do. From the start point, the tracker will study the sign and commit it to memory. The tracker must be able to recognize the same sign repeatedly as well as notice discrepancies in the sign and track picture.
- Formulate a profile of the quarry by interpreting the signs he leaves behind. The tracker is always looking to answer questions such as: Is the quarry tired and lazy or alert and confident? He recognizes indicators of the morale and discipline of the quarry. By observing *all* sign, the tracker develops a "track picture" that allows him to determine and anticipate the quarry's actions.
- Anticipate where the tracks are heading and the quarry's intentions.
- Locate the quarry.

CHARACTERISTICS OF A COMBAT TRACKER

Any person can become track aware and learn how to track with some proficiency. Not every individual, however, possesses the characteristics required to perform the duties of a combat tracker or serve as a member of a combat tracker unit. To produce an effective combat tracker, an organization must not take an "assembly-line approach" to the selection and training of individuals to perform combat tracking operations. A combat tracker cannot be mass-produced instantly; effective training takes time, and quality is always better than quantity.

A combat tracker is a member of a cohesive and well-disciplined unit whose primary mission is to hunt down an individual who is likely armed, dangerous, and more familiar with the terrain and environment than the tracker squad is.

A tracker must possess certain qualities essential to the successful performance of his duties.

- Honesty to himself and to others
- Patience and perseverance
- An analytical and inquisitive mind that continuously seeks out information about the enemy and operational environment
- Acute sensory skills and an intense attention to detail
- Mental and physical toughness
- Personal initiative
- Aggressiveness and tenacity
- An attitude of self-reliance
- Tactical and technical proficiency
- Excellent fieldcraft and bushcraft skills
- An understanding of the big picture and the part the tracker plays in it

The better the tracker understands the enemy, his habits, traits, and tactics, as well as his motives and aspirations, the greater the tracker's tactical advantage over his enemy will be. When properly selected and trained, the tracker will be a much greater asset for gathering information, finding the enemy, or recovering lost or missing personnel than any piece of technology or hardware. History has proven that when trackers are organized into cohesive tracker squads and platoons, larger combat units such as battalions and brigades increase their operational and war-fighting capabilities exponentially.

USING AVAILABLE LIGHT

When learning to track for the first time, it is important to understand how to use available light to the best advantage. Light is one of the most important requirements for effective tracking: In fact, light (and shadow) will determine whether the tracker is able to observe sign or not.

As the sun rises, it casts long shadows that bring out the details of any impression made on the ground. As the sun climbs, these details will gradually fade. At noon, when the sun is directly over-

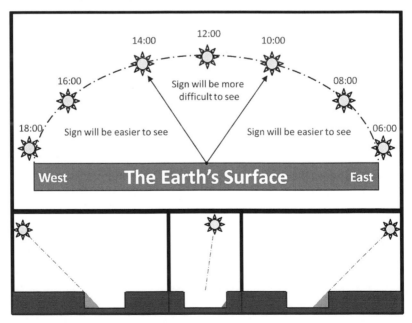

head, little or no shadow will appear, and impression details will become almost invisible. As the sun begins to fall, the shadows again lengthen, bringing details into sharper relief.

To best use available light, the tracker needs to be positioned so that the tracks he's observing are between him and the light source. Facing in the direction of the sun will enhance the shadows, making track details easier to see. While following the tracks, the tracker should always be aware of his position relative to the track line and the sun. The tracker may have to move around the tracks to keep the track line between him and the sun—the best angle for viewing. He must be careful, though, not to contaminate the track line as he moves. If the tracker is following impressions that run directly away from the sun, he may need to stand to the side of the track line and look back over his shoulder.

When the tracker is confronted with poor lighting conditions (such as underneath a dense forest canopy), he may be able to overcome the lack of natural light by using an artificial light source (a flashlight, for instance, or a signal mirror to deflect light). He can then manipulate the light source to create the best angle to view the tracks.

SIGN

Sign is any evidence of disturbance created within the natural state of the environment by the passage of human, animal, or machinery. Although sign is visible, people often don't recognize it because they don't know what they are looking at. In fact, it is frequently overlooked and considered by some in the law enforcement community to be "missed evidence."

The tracker must be able to identify sign within any environment in order to locate the quarry. Humans and animals may contaminate an area prior to or after the quarry's passing, and so the tracker must be able to work through any contamination and identify what sign belongs to the quarry and what sign does not. To do so, the tracker classifies all sign into one of two categories: conclusive or inconclusive.

Conclusive sign is the evidence that is positively connected to or associated with the quarry (full or partial footprints, for example, or litter). Typically, the tracker will find conclusive footprint evi-

dence in a "track trap," which is anything that will hold an impression left by the quarry. Good track traps include soft or muddy patches of ground; steep slopes; banks of rivers and streams; the sides of paved roads or on dirt roads, paths, and game trails; the edges of clearings, plantations, and flat ground; and any obstacle that must be crossed or that causes channelization of the quarry's route.

Inconclusive sign cannot be confirmed as belonging to the quarry but, with other evidence taken into account, could have been made by the quarry (trampled grass or vegetation, for example).

VISUAL TRACKING INDICATORS

The ability to recognize sign is crucial to being able to track effectively. The tracker who can correctly identify the basic characteristics of sign will be able to track successfully in any environment. Visual tracking indicators are recognized by a number of characteristics.

Regularity. A regular pattern might be straight lines or geometrical shapes pressed into the earth's surface—impressions typically not found in nature.

Regularity

Flattening. The pressure of an object compresses an area, causing flattening to occur within the natural environment, which creates a contrast with the surrounding area. (If the ground is hard and the tracker isn't sure if observed flattening could

Flattening

Transfer

Color change

Disturbance

Litter

have been caused by the quarry, the tracker should test the ground next to the questionable sign by trying to flatten the ground in a similar manner. If the impressions do not look alike, the tracker can rule out that the flat spot was made by the quarry.)

Transfer and Transference. The deposit of material carried from one environmental medium to another can serve as a clue to the quarry's presence and movements.

Color Change. A difference in color or texture from the natural color of the surrounding area is also a valuable indicator.

Disturbance. The passage of the quarry often causes an alteration, rearrangement, or movement of objects from their usual position within their natural state.

Litter. Any object that has been discarded intentionally or unintentionally should be noted and observed carefully.

VISUAL INDICATORS

Visual tracking indicators can be grouped into a number of different categories based on location and type.

GROUND INDICATORS

Ground indicators are those detected below the ankle line. Some examples include:

- Footprints
- Vehicular track or tire tread impressions
- Boot scuffs
- Turned-over dead leaves (which will show a darker color after being disturbed)
- Broken cobwebs
- Crushed twigs or leaves on the ground
- Trampled grass pointing in the direction the quarry traveled
- Morning dew rubbed off by the quarry's passage
- Bruised vegetation
- Scuffed or scraped tree roots
- Disturbed insect life on the ground
- Disturbed grass, leaves, or ground vegetation
- Mud, soil, sand, or water transferred from footwear onto another medium
- Kicked or turned-over embedded material (rocks, stones, dead branches, and so on)
- Fallen twigs or broken branches
- Stones or rocks on the sides of hills moved slightly or rolled away after being stepped on (whether the track leads up or down the slope)
- Stones on a loose or soft surface pressed into the ground or holes where stones have been pushed below the surface
- Moss scraped off rocks or stones by a boot or hand
- Footprints on stream banks or in shallow water
- Mud stirred up and discolored water

- Rocks splashed with water
- Disturbed mud or grass or other vegetation at the edge of waterways

AERIAL INDICATORS

Aerial indicators are found above ankle height. Some examples include:

- Tall grass or vegetation pushed down into an unnatural position
- Broken cobwebs
- Tunnels through vegetation made low to the ground
- Marks on the sides of logs that lie across a path
- Detached or missing leaves
- Disturbed branches pointing in the quarry's direction of movement
- Green leaves of bushes pushed aside and twisted, showing the undersides, which will usually be lighter than the tops
- Vines dragged forward in the quarry's direction of travel
- Scratches or scuffs on trees trunks
- Bark scraped off trees where they were used as handholds when the quarry was going uphill or where equipment (such as a tarp or hammock) was tied
- Changes in color and unnatural position of vegetation
- Cut or broken vegetation

LITTER INDICATORS

Litter indicators are any object that's been discarded intentionally or unintentionally. Some examples include:

- Cigarettes butts
- Toilet paper
- Candy wrappers
- Equipment and gear
- Used batteries

- Food containers
- Ammo packaging
- Spent ammo casings
- Used medical supplies
- Beverage containers
- Chewing tobacco, gum, or candy

BLOOD INDICATORS

Arterial blood is highly oxygenated and bright red in color. Such blood spurts from a wound at regular intervals. Arterial blood sign associated with the quarry shows that a life-threatening wound was inflicted. Even if properly treated immediately, the quarry will most likely weaken if on the run and need to rest often. He will likely die without advanced medical care.

Venous blood leaks from a wound in a generally constant manner, resulting in a dark red trail of drops. Usually, this type of wound is not life threatening, and the wounded quarry would still be able to move long distances. If the wound is untreated, however, the quarry may slow down over time because of blood loss.

Wounds to the lungs often result in a pink frothy blood trail, often accompanied by phlegm clots. The movements of a quarry so wounded would be limited, and he would require assistance from others. Abdominal wounds may show blood mixed with digestive fluids that gives off an odor and is light in color. Severe head injuries usually result in heavy, slimy, glutinous blood deposits—a quarry so wounded may not be able to travel very far.

Remember that all blood sign is affected by air, sun, and time: Its color will change. Initially, when blood is fresh, it will be bright in color; as time progresses, it will turn to a dark brown or rust color as the moisture from the blood evaporates.

The tracker must be extra cautious when following a blood trail. If a wounded enemy faces imminent death, he may set an ambush and attempt to take out as many of his pursuers as possible before he dies.

BODILY DISCHARGE INDICATORS

Bodily discharge indicators are materials discharged from the body. Spittle may tell the tracker that the quarry chews or dips tobacco or was eating sunflower or pumpkin seeds, for example. It could also indicate that the quarry used a particular spot to brush his or her teeth. Mucus may tell the tracker that the quarry has a cold or allergy. Vomit may tell the tracker that the quarry is suffering from an illness. Urine, by the color, smell, or amount, may indicate whether the quarry is hydrated or dehydrated. Typically someone who is dehydrated will have darker-colored urine than one who is hydrated; urine from a dehydrated person will also have a more potent ammonia smell than urine from a hydrated person. The amount of urine can also provide clues. The placement of the urine stain together with the placement of the quarry's foot impressions can also indicate whether the quarry is male or female (men will typically stand when urinating while women squat in a field environment). Feces can provide information about the quarry's diet, whether the quarry is local to the area or not, and if he or she is sick or healthy.

ANIMAL INDICATORS

Visual indicators of animals could be associated with a quarry, especially if the quarry is using the animal as a method of transportation (riding a horse, for example, or using a mule or camel to transport material) or traveling with a pet such as a dog.

Signs that local wildlife has been disturbed can also indicate a quarry's presence or passing. These indicators include animals that are spooked and flee from their original position or animals that howl or fall silent when intruders move through their territory.

NON-VISUAL INDICATORS

In addition to visual tracking indicators, olfactory and auditory indicators offer valuable clues to the conscientious tracker. *Olfactory indicators* are those that can be smelled. They include smoke, cooking odors, body odors, scents from soap and other toiletries, freshly dug earth, tobacco smoke, latrines or feces, and chemical odors.

Auditory indicators are those indicators that can be heard. They include talking, whispering, laughing, coughing, and sneezing; banging and clattering; movement through brush; vehicle engine noises; generator noises; gunfire; and the abrupt beginning or ending of insect and animal sounds.

FACTORS THAT AFFECT SIGN

A number of factors affect the appearance of sign made by the quarry. All are interrelated, and the tracker must be aware of how each might affect the others.

CONTAMINATION

Following the quarry's sign is the tracker's most important task. To do this, the tracker must be aware of possible contamination by other sources of sign, including wildlife in the area. The tracker must be able to differentiate between the sign of animals and that of the quarry.

He must also be aware of possible contamination from other humans in the area. If there is "extra" man-made sign visible, the tracker must be able to distinguish the quarry's sign from that made by others. Collecting and recording detailed information about the quarry's footprints and other sign allow him to do this effectively.

TERRAIN

Tracking may be conducted on any terrain, so the tracker must have a comprehensive knowledge of what type of sign will be created within each type of environment he's likely to encounter.

Grassland. When the quarry passes through 2- to 3-foot-high grass, the track line will be fairly easy to follow. High grass that's been pushed down will stay down for some time, depending on the weather conditions and the type of grass it is. Grass that is pushed down by a passerby will point in the direction of travel and display a color change known as shine or blaze that will stand out against the surrounding undisturbed grasses. As well, if dew accumulated the night before, it will likely be rubbed off.

Mud, dirt, and sand may also be transferred from the quarry's footwear to the grass. If the grass is dry, broken and crushed stems will be visible. Footprints might also be detected underneath dry grass. In short grass (12 inches or less), the steps of the quarry will damage the grass, and the ground may capture a footprint impression.

Rocky Areas. Tracking through rocky areas is not as difficult as it might seem. Rocks are easily disturbed, displaced, and scuffed by a person's passage. Unless the quarry is moving over large boulders, stones and rocks will either be pressed into the ground or moved from their original positions. Stones pressed into the ground leave either a ridge around their edges where mud is forced out or, in drier soil, cracks in the ground. Stones and rocks on the sides of inclines will almost always be disturbed and displaced when traveled over, whether the quarry is moving up or downhill. Soil disturbed by the quarry's passage will also show a distinct color change, and it will often capture some type of impression.

If the quarry climbs over large rocks, his footwear may scratch the surface, depending on the type of footwear worn. If the quarry climbs over sandstone, his footwear may make dark-colored scratches; if he climbs over lava rock, it will create light scratches. Moss- or lichen-covered rocks will be easily and distinctly damaged when a person climbs over them.

If stones are brittle and crack, crumble, or chip, fragments will be usually be visible after someone passes over them. Small stones that get caught in the soles of a person's footwear can be deposited further down the trail and show up against a different medium.

Primary Forests. A quarry moving through primary forest will likely leave behind numerous clues to his passage. Leaves disturbed on the forest floor will appear darker than those that are undisturbed. Dry twigs and leaves will crack or break under the pressure of a person walking over them. Broken sticks and twigs can help the tracker assess the age of a track, too. Freshly broken twigs, whether dead or alive, will appear lighter at the break. This will darken with age. The tracker can break the twig again and conduct a comparison to determine whether the sign is old or fresh.

Where undergrowth is thick, the quarry may have to push through the vegetation, exposing the lighter undersides of leaves. Green, freshly broken limbs will usually have an odor, which dissipates over time. Again, a comparison can be made.

Logs or fallen trees that have been stepped on may have bark scraped off. If the quarry stepped over rather than on a log, impressions may be found on either side of the log. Large tree roots that are stepped on will often show signs of bruising and may have bark scuffed off.

Broken cobwebs across a path may indicate the quarry's passage, even indicating how recently he passed—spiders typically spin webs at night.

Secondary Forests. When primary growth has been cleared, secondary growth begins. Typically, this growth is thick and difficult to move through. To do so, the quarry may have to cut through it or crawl. Signs of the quarry's passage may include broken branches and twigs, leaves knocked off branches, branches pushed forward in the direction of travel, footprints or other marks along the ground surface, tunnels made low to the ground through extremely thick vegetation, broken cobwebs, and aerial sign in the form of scuffed tree bark on limbs.

Swamps and Other Wet Areas. Sign left by a quarry moving through wet areas include footprints along the banks of waterways, in shallow water with little or no current, or in mud; discolored water from mud or a stirred-up streambed as well as a color change in the water indicating where the quarry crossed; and water splashed on rocks. Impressions will be made in mud at the point of entry, and water will be transferred onto the ground at the point of exit.

In mangrove or similar swamps, clouds of mud will be stirred up by the quarry's passage and branches will be bent where the quarry used them for handholds. Tall grass and reeds along the water's edge will be pushed aside at entry and exit points.

Sandy Areas. Sand is easy to track on. If the sand surface is moderately hard, the footprint impression will appear clear. If the sand surface is soft, the footprint will be deep and may have little or no detail. The biggest problem the tracker may encounter when tracking on sand is that rain and wind can obliterate impressions quickly.

WEATHER CONDITIONS

The weather can have a dramatic effect on visible sign, and the tracker must be aware of how weather conditions can affect clues left by the quarry.

Direct Sunlight. The sun's heat will accelerate the color change of sign in exposed areas. An impression made in mud can remain for some time after it has dried. In softer soil, however, the edges of a drying impression will begin to erode. As well, green vegetation pushed down by the quarry will spring back to its normal position relatively quickly when warmed by the sun. Tree and brush limbs broken by the quarry will dry out and turn brown in sunlight at the point of the break.

Wind. Disturbed vegetation will be affected by wind, returning back to its normal position more quickly and thus concealing ground sign. Footprint appearance can also be affected by wind: Wind blowing over impressions will smooth over the edges and blow debris into them.

Precipitation. Precipitation can be the tracker's worst enemy. Rain will wash away most disturbances caused by the quarry and generally destroy most sign. It also will cause vegetation to return to its natural state more quickly. Snow can partially fill or completely obliterate footprints and other sign, depending on how deep the impression is and the amount of snow that falls.

WILDLIFE
The wildlife that inhabits an area can either help or hinder a combat tracking operation. Birds, insects, and other animals will alert others—both other animals and people—of an intruder in their midst. (Some monkeys and birds, for example, will sound a warning when an intruder enters their territory; insects, on the other hand, will go silent.) Understanding the habits of the wildlife in the area of operations will without a doubt assist the tracker. Of course, a habitat that is home to large populations of wildlife (or domestic animals such as cattle, goats, or sheep) will likely be a place where human sign is quickly contaminated, so much so that effective tracking becomes almost impossible.

THE AGE OF SIGN
The passage of time is one of the most important considerations in tracking, and aging sign accurately is one of the tracker's biggest challenges. The colder the track is, the more difficult it will be to follow. Only experience and practice will help overcome the challenges of determining the age of sign and tracking sign that has aged significantly.

ESTIMATING AGE
To determine the age of sign, the tracker should have a good knowledge of the local weather conditions and their effects on

Footprint impression made after a rainstorm

soil and vegetation as well as on man-made items that may have been left by the quarry. A number of factors need to be considered.

Rain. If the track was found during midday, and it had rained at 5 o'clock in the morning but the track is clear, the track had to have made after the rain—sometime between five and noon. If tracks show pockmarks inside them—indications of rainfall—they were made before or during the last rain.

Foliage. Some foliage that's been broken or bruised can begin to die in a matter of minutes once exposed to the sun. Any unnatural state and position of vegetation should be noted—practice and experience will teach the tracker how to recognize the factors that will allow him to determine the age of the track.

Prints in mud. The dryness of a track in mud or soft ground is important. If the track is very fresh, water will not have run back into it. Within minutes, however, water will run back into it and any mud that has been pushed up around the edges, as well as mud kicked forward of the print, will begin to dry out.

Superimposed game tracks. Most wild animals lie up during the day and move at night. If the quarry's impressions have animal tracks superimposed on them, then the quarry's prints were made during the previous night.

Leaves covering tracks. The number of leaves that fall on to a track depends on the type of leaf as well as the amount of rain or wind that has occurred within the area. This may indicate the age of the track.

Objects associated with humans. Objects found by the tracker along the track, at a rest halt, or in a campsite will help him determine the age of a track. When moving through an area, people will typically take with them many man-made objects: clothing, medical supplies, camping or sleeping equipment, weapons and ammunition, luxury items, and, possibly, communications equipment.

If the tracker locates litter from these man-made objects while conducting the operation he will need to know how these objects are affected by the ageing process. The tracker needs to know the type, purpose, origin, and possibly the manufacturer of the product in order to estimate the age for items such as paper products, cloth products, plastic products as well as food and food containers. Food products will spoil and decay. Items with color will fade over time when exposed to sunlight.

AGING STANDS
A good way to learn how to estimate age is to build an aging stand—a tracker's "science project" that he checks periodically over

a period of a week or two to note how both shaded items and items in direct sunlight age over a given period of time. Just like a sniper who creates a sniper log for weather, winds, altitude, temperature, and ballistics data that will affect his shot, a
tracker notes how a variety of objects age in a certain area. It's an effective way to get "acclimated" for tracking in any particular region.

The aging stand should be large enough for the tracker to walk around and observe the items without contaminating the area. Tested items can include paper products (newspaper, paper bags, copy and writing paper, toilet paper, and paper napkins), food (canned meat, cooked and uncooked rice, bread, fruits, nuts, and vegetables—these should be opened with some of the food left in the container and some spilled out over the ground), drink containers (plastic, glass, and metal cups, bottles, and cans with some of the contents spilled on the ground), human waste (urine, feces, and spit), tobacco products, and blood and medical litter (blood, bandages, medical tape, aspirin, and IV trash).

Broken limbs and foliage left at the stand will show how limbs brown and vegetation withers. Tracks made with boots, tennis shoes, and bare feet and ammo cartridges, expended ammo casings, machine gun links, and ammunition packaging are also useful things to age and observe.

The tracker can also create a fire pit that is large enough and hot enough to boil water and cook food then see how it ages; he can also dig a hole and leave it exposed and dig another and bury an object to resemble an anti-personnel or anti-tank mine.

2

Human Gait, Tracks, and Track Interpretation

By studying and understanding the elements of an individual's gait the tracker will be able to determine whether the quarry is running, walking, carrying weight, or traveling in a straight line or turning, as well as whether he is healthy or injured (an injury to the foot, back, hip, knee, leg, or ankle will cause the individual to move differently and change the pressure exerted on weight-bearing areas of the foot).

KEY ELEMENTS OF GAIT

There are several key elements associated with an individual's gait that a tracker should identify, analyze, and record. All of the elements are interconnected: Every time one of them changes, it will affect the appearance of the others. When this occurs, the tracker should quickly analyze the signs and develop a picture of what occurred to cause the change.

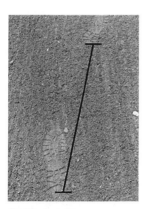

Stride length. Stride length is the linear distance of one step. It is measured from the rear edge of the heel impression of the rear foot to the rear edge of the heel impression of the forward foot. The quarry's stride length will indicate the rate at which he is moving. The greater the distance between foot impressions, the faster the individual is moving. The shorter the

Stride length

21

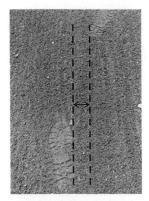

Stride width

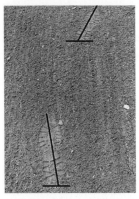

Foot angle

Pressure

distance, the slower he is moving. Short stride lengths can also indicate that the quarry is carrying weight.

Stride width. Stride width is the perpendicular distance between left and right foot impressions. It is measured from the inside edges of two opposite heel impressions. A narrow stride width may indicate that an individual is carrying weight—attempting to balance the load over the legs, narrowing the stride width. A common misconception is that the stride width of an individual carrying a heavy load will always widen. This might happen, but a wide stride might just as likely be caused by a rash or chaffing on the quarry's inner thighs.

Foot Angle. Foot angle is the angular measurement of the midline of the foot in relation to the direction of travel. Foot angle indicates to a tracker whether the quarry is traveling in a straight line, is about to turn, or has turned and changed direction.

Pressure. As the quarry places his foot on the ground, a certain amount of weight is distributed over that surface. When the quarry moves in a particular direction, more pressure is exerted on that side of the foot than the other. When this occurs, the depth of the impression and movement of soil and ground cover around the impression will give the tracker a clue as to what action took place. Analyzing an impression and the amount of pressure that was exerted may tell the tracker the direction his quarry is moving in or whether the quarry is carrying weight.

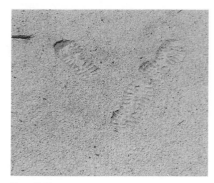

Dwell Time. This is the amount of time the quarry appears to have remained idle within a given area.

Dwell time

THREE PHASES OF A FOOTSTEP

The scientific community typically identifies two phases of a human gait: the *stance phase* and the *swing phase.* For tracking, the three subphases of the stance phase are the most important. Interpreting these subphases will help the tracker identify the quarry's unique foot movement characteristics, which aids in distinguishing the quarry's footprints from others and identifying the activities carried out by the quarry, such as walking forwards or backwards, jogging, and running.

The *contact phase* is the first part of the sequence of a footstep. It begins when the foot initially makes contact with the ground and continues until the foot is flat on the ground.

The *mid-stance phase* is when body weight passes over the foot as the body is in motion. During mid-stance the foot is supporting an individual's body weight and moving forward in the direction of travel. This phase ends when the individual's body weight moves forward enough to cause

Contact phase

Mid-stance phase

Propulsion phase

Weight distribution pattern

the contact point to rise slightly off the ground.

The *propulsion phase* is the last phase of the sequence. It's when the foot pushes off the ground to propel the body in the direction of travel.

A specific pattern of weight distribution occurs when a person takes a step. At first, the heel will make contact with the ground and begin to absorb the weight of the individual's body. As the body's momentum continues forward, body weight is absorbed and distributed along the outside part of the foot to the ball of the foot. The pattern ends when the big toe pushes off. (If the individual is walking backwards, the process is reversed.)

IDENTIFYING AND RECORDING TRACKS

It is impossible for a human to walk anywhere without leaving some sign of their passage. Each time an individual takes a step the pressure from their foot will create some kind of impression or disturbance. Careful observation of the details of a disturbance or impression should reveal what type of footwear made the impression and the individual characteristics of the person who made it. Sometimes partial prints will be found; at other times, only disturbances within the natural environment will be seen. If a tracker is really lucky, he might find a fully detailed footprint impression. Such an impression is the best conclusive evidence that links the sign to the quarry.

Footprint impressions can lead the tracker to the quarry's location or provide specific information about him and his habits. Identifying and confirming the correct tracks left by the quarry is a continuous process that the tracker performs throughout a tracking mission.

When the tracker is assessing a track, he should ask himself a number of questions:

- Is the impression the left or right foot?
- What type of footwear made the impression (boot, shoe, sandal)?
- Is the sole flat or semi-flat, or does it have a pronounced heel?
- Is the toe rounded, square, or pointed?
- What type of sole is it (casual, athletic, work-type)?
- What is the pattern of the sole?
- Are any manufacturer or sizing labels apparent?
- Is there a pattern and, if so, is it regular or irregular?
- Does the pattern include shapes such as diamonds, circles, half circles, squares, ripples, or bars?
- Does it have a lugged border?
- If so, is it straight or curved?
- Are there any unique wear patterns that make the impression stand out?

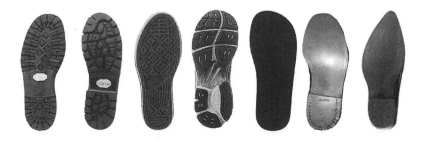

A useful technique is for the tracker to give the quarry a nickname based on his footprint characteristics. For example, if the track impression left by the quarry has an obvious zigzag pattern then the quarry's nickname could be Zigzag. Giving each quarry a nickname helps the tracker individually identify and profile each person he is following. When communicating information to other elements of the operation, every element will be able to identify the person or persons by their nickname.

A footprint ID card allows the tracker to record detailed information about the impressions made by the quarry that will be vital to the conduct of the mission. Once the tracker identifies the quarry's sign, he should record the current time, the location of the impression, nickname assigned to the quarry, and the quarry's direction of travel. This information should be noted as soon as possible. A sketch of the characteristics of the impression is also useful to help tracker commit the impression to memory as well as provide details for other trackers.

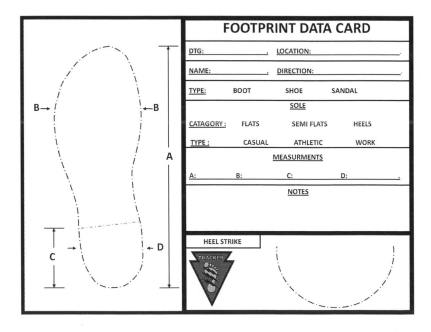

As well, the following measurements should be taken with a tape measure and recorded: length of the entire print from the rear edge of the heel to the tip of the toe, width of the widest portion of the sole, heel length, and heel width.

Length of footprint (A)

Remember that if only partial impressions were made, details of only the partial impression should be recorded. *Do not invent evidence to fill in the blanks.* Record only what can be observed. If new evidence is discovered later then the appropriate blanks can be filled in.

Width of ball of foot (B)

BAREFOOT IMPRESSIONS

Each person's foot is unique. Over time, the length and width of the foot and the shape and placement of the pads of the toes, ball of the foot, and heel can change because of the type of shoes worn, activities engaged in, or injuries suffered. All have an impact on the characteristics of an individual's feet.

Length of heel (C)

The size, shape, and contour features of a bare footprint will

Width of heel (D)

be distinctive, just as fingerprints are. If the quarry is walking bare-foot, it is important for a tracker to be able to identify him by the various features of the foot, such as the number of toes; toe line; contours and features of the individual toes, ball of the foot, arch, and heel; and any pits, cracks, scars, or deformities.

A complete bare footprint impression consists of five toe impressions and impressions of the ball of the foot, the arch, and the heel. The size, orientation, and shape of these characteristics can provide the tracker with useful clues to establish the quarry's identity.

Bare foot characteristics are broken down into four categories:

Toe Area. The positions of the toes relative to each other is often a key identifying characteristic. They can be aligned straight or randomly or be arranged like a staircase. The length of the toes, distance between them, and number of toes are also unique characteristics. Deformities can be indicated by the toes' positions. The presence or lack of toe impressions can indicate characteristics such as missing digits, curly toe, claw toe, mallet toe, and hammer toe, or surgically altered or congenitally defective toes (a bifid fifth toe, for example). The tracker must consider whether the absence of toe impressions is due to missing toes or to some deformity or injury that prevents the toes from coming into contact with the ground.

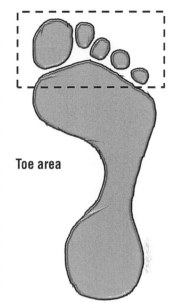

Toe area

Impressions made by feet that have never worn shoes are commonly found to have the toes in alignment with their respective metatarsals, giving the foot a fan-shaped appearance. They also generally have toes in alignment with the longitudinal axis of the rear foot.

Ball of the Foot. The ball of the foot is the padded area that extends from the first tarsal to the outside edge of the foot. Unique features such as pits, creases, scars, and, especially, bunions are often visible in ball impressions. Bunions can occur on

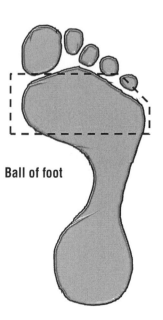

Ball of foot

both sides of the feet; they are caused by pressure of the sides of shoes on foot joints, which causes a deformity. Bunions appear as an extension of the ball beyond its usual confines when compared with the confines of the toes.

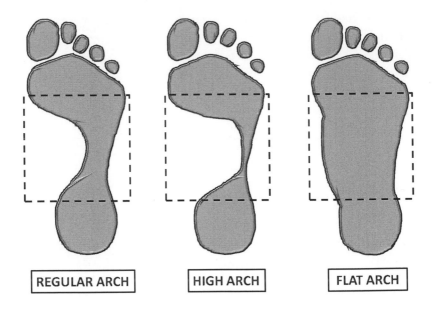

| REGULAR ARCH | HIGH ARCH | FLAT ARCH |

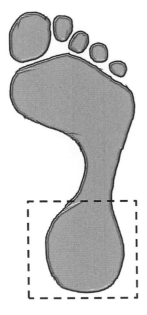

Heel

Foot Arch. A foot that has a high arch will leave less of an impression than one with a normal or flattened arch. People who have never worn shoes for most of their lives are likely to be flat-footed.

Heel. The heel will also have different sizes and shapes: long, short, wide, narrow, round, or oval. The heel area often shows the presence of unusual features such as pits, creases, or scars.

The tracker will rarely see full footprint impressions. Instead, he will track by following partial prints, flat impressions, scuffs, or disturbed vegetation. The tracker may have to follow inconclusive sign before finding conclusive sign that positively identifies the quarry. When conclusive sign is found, the tracker should identify it to his team leader as the "last known sign" (LKS). It's the team leader's responsibility to protect the sign from contamination as well as to mark and record it. If the tracker inadvertently follows the wrong set of tracks for a significant distance, the team will know where to return in order to correct the error.

PRINCIPLES OF TRACKING

These seven basic principles will help the tracker when following a set of tracks.

- Positively identify the tracks you're going to follow.
- Keep the track line between you and the light source.
- Observe and track as far out as the sign can be recognized.
- Never move further than the last known sign.
- Never contaminate the sign.
- Never track faster than your abilities allow.
- Get into the mind of the quarry.

ESTIMATING QUARRY GROUP SIZE

Whenever possible, trackers must assess and reassess the number of quarry being pursued. An accurate estimate will allow higher command to commit an adequate amount of resources to the operation. One of the best places to determine the size of the enemy is where the group conducted a rest halt or camped for the night. Carefully counting individual resting positions will give the tracker a good estimate of the group's size.

If the track line leads to a rest stop, take time to observe all sign to ensure that the location isn't also where the group has split up. If it appears that the enemy has split into smaller groups, the team leader may want to identify nearby villages. If the track line splits and appears to be going in several directions toward a populated area, the incident may have been conducted by locals who are now proceeding back to their respective villages. If the track line is heading toward a border or unpopulated area, the enemy could be a more organized element that is moving to a base camp or safe haven. If the amount of sign discovered at the rest area is greater than the amount of sign that lead you there, there's the possibility that more than one group may have been involved in the initial incident or are operating in the area.

To determine the size of a moving group, the tracker must first find a track trap. The tracker will then be able to determine or confirm the size of the group by using one of the following methods.

Direct count method

DIRECT COUNT METHOD
The direct count method is used when all foot impressions have individual distinctive characteristics that can be easily differentiated. The various tracks are simply counted. This method is typically accurate for up to five people.

AVERAGE PACE METHOD
The average pace method is used when a key print has been identified. A key print is one with a distinctive sole, wear pattern, and/or features. The key print is usually made by the last person within a group and will be the clearest and most distinct footprint.

Draw a line behind the first key print identified and another line at the middle of the very next print made by the same foot. Count *all the prints* between the two lines, including any that may fall on the lines themselves. Divide the number by 2. (If the number counted is odd, always round up before dividing by 2.) This will give you a good estimate of the number of people in the quarry group.

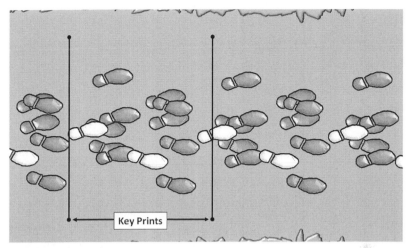

Average pace method

BOX METHOD

The box method is used when no key prints can be identified. Draw a line behind one print, measure 48 inches forward, and draw another line. Count *all full and partial prints* between the two lines (round up if the number is odd), then divide by 2.

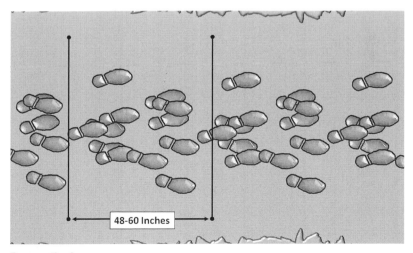

Box method

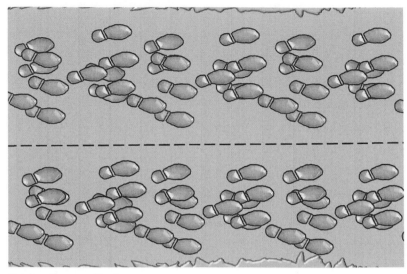

Comparison method

COMPARISON METHOD
The comparison method is used when a large group has walked in rough single file and the tracks have been superimposed on top of one another. The only way the tracker can estimate the number within the group is to reproduce the amount of sign and compare both track lines side by side. If possible, use an area next to the quarry's sign that is approximately the same width. The team leader and the tracker will attempt to recreate the amount of sign by walking over the test area. One of the team members will count how

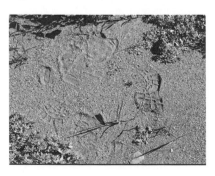

many times it takes to recreate the same amount of sign as the quarry group. (It's a good idea to add 5 if the count is over 30.)

ACTIVITY INDICATORS
Activity indicators are marks and impressions that show that a certain activity has taken

place. By analyzing and interpreting these marks and impressions, the tracker can make educated assumptions about the quarry's behavior. This will help the tracker understand the quarry as well as anticipate what he might do next. Information that can be gained from interpreting activity indicators include:

- Speed and direction
- Number in quarry group
- Age and gender of quarry
- Physical condition and disabilities
- Attempts to camouflage tracks
- State of training, discipline, and morale
- Weight carried
- Whether the quarry is lost or confused
- Whether the quarry is determined and focused
- Whether the quarry is armed
- Whether the quarry is moving tactically
- Whether the quarry is security conscious
- Whether the quarry was traversing up or downhill
- Whether the quarry was moving during the day or night
- If and when the quarry rested
- Direction the quarry is traveling and where he came from

Activity indicators, when interpreted together with other information gathered along the track line, can provide information related to the larger tactical or operational picture:
- Infiltration and exfiltration corridors and methods
- Methods of resupply
- Safe areas and support bases that may be used routinely (a piece of ground that provides water, cover, and concealment, for example, or individual safe houses or areas where there may be local support)
- Cultural or religious affiliations
- Campsites and patrol bases
- Cache sites

- Observation and surveillance locations
- Potential reconnaissance of ambush or attack positions
- Type of equipment employed

ESTIMATING RATE OF MOVEMENT

Analyzing the stride of the quarry will help the tracker estimate the quarry's rate of movement. To do this, measure the length of one stride, from the rear edge of the heel of the first key print (the right footprint, for example) to the rear edge of the heel of the opposite key print (the next left footprint). The average walking step length is 30 inches. If the track shows prints that are a greater distance apart than the normal walking step, then the quarry is likely jogging or running. (Keep in mind that the quarry's height will affect his stride—a 6-foot-tall man's stride while walking will be longer than that of a 5½-foot-tall man.)

Additionally, if the impressions of the ball and toe of the foot are pronounced, and there is scuffed earth to the rear and front of the impressions, then the quarry has increased his speed. As well, ground sign such as forcefully broken twigs, torn and twisted vegetation, branches roughly pushed aside, and young vegetation that's crushed, flattened, or bruised will indicate that the quarry is moving quickly.

DETERMINING IF A LOAD IS BEING CARRIED

If the sign the tracker is following appears to be deep and the stride is shorter than normal, the quarry might be carrying something weighty, such as a backpack. If good impressions can be identified, the tracker can create his own impression next to the quarry's and compare the depths of the two.

Other clues can help determine if the quarry is carrying a load.

- The heavier the load, the less spring in the step. Full footprints will be observed rather than partial impressions.
- The distance between steps as well as the stride width may be shorter than those of someone who isn't carrying weight.

- There will be a greater number of full-print impressions made, and the heel will be very obvious.
- The quarry will take a deliberate approach to crossing or negotiating obstacles.
- When the track leads up or down a hill or embankment, the quarry carrying a load will take greater care placing his feet in order to keep his balance; he will also likely use multiple handholds to help him up or down.
- The width and amount of shoulder-high vegetation disturbance will indicate if a quarry is carrying a load—the load will catch on vegetation and cause leaves to be stripped from branches and vines to be pulled in the direction of movement.
- Where the quarry takes a break, he might set down what he is carrying, and the object may flatten dirt and vegetation. If the ground is soft enough, the weight of the object might leave an identifiable impression.

LEARNING HOW TO TRACK

In learning how to track, the most important factor is learning to become *track aware* by detecting each sign, no matter how small. A good way to do this is by practicing the step-by-step method—detecting and studying a single step, followed by every successive step, focusing on the disturbances made in the natural environment.

To practice this drill, select a patch of flat ground about 10 yards by 20 yards (roughly the size of a volleyball court). This will serve as your "tracking box." The ground within the box should be soft enough to capture a track line over its entire length. If necessary, the ground in the box can be raked to loosen up the surface a bit. Walk through the box to lay out a track line, or have someone else do it.

First identify both key prints of a step—one left and one right foot print in succession. Measure the length of the step by noting the distance from the heel of the rear key print to the heel on the forward key print. (For measuring, a 12-foot retractable metal measuring tape that is rigid and can lock when extended works best.)

Extend the tape measure from the heel of the rear key print and place the end of the tape measure even with the heel of the forward key print. The curved rear edge of the heel is likely the part that's most prominent. Measure the stride and lock the tape.

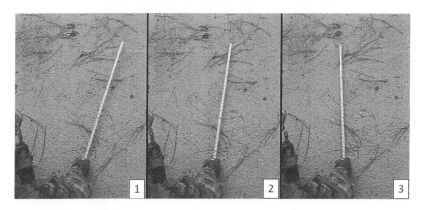

To determine where the next step landed, move the measuring tape body so it is just above the rear edge of the heel of the forward key print. Swing the tip of the locked tape in an arc that covers the area where the next step should have landed. This arc will help you focus on a small piece of ground rather than a large area.

Sweep the tip of the tape slowly, studying the ground directly in front of the tip for sign. Sweep from a two o'clock position to a ten o'clock position, focusing on the left, for the left footprint; for the right footprint sweep from ten o'clock to two o'clock, focusing on the right. Somewhere within the arc the tip of the tape measure will swing above the heel of where the next footstep landed. (Remember that at times a person's stride may vary by as much as 6 inches.)

Proceed forward, finding and observing each step in sequence until you reach the end of the box. Go slowly. Your objective in this drill is not to track and hunt down a quarry; it is to learn how to detect sign.

COMBAT TRACKING

With practice, your abilities to detect and follow sign will improve. The next step is to work on a more aggressive method for use in combat conditions. The combat tracking method forces the tracker to observe as far ahead as he can recognize the sign while steadily moving forward.

The purpose of this is to follow the track line quicker to close the time-distance gap, and to make the tracker more situationally aware of the operational environment and prevent him from triggering booby traps or walking into an ambush. It also facilitates better visual contact with team members who are providing security.

Focusing only on tracks near your feet has some negative effects: It causes tunnel vision and eyestrain; it creates poor situational awareness, which makes the tracker and his squad susceptible to enemy ambush; and the process is time consuming and could allow the quarry to evade pursuers.

Track Pursuit Drill. The tracker most likely will be pursuing an enemy who is armed, dangerous, and knows the operational area better than the tracker does. To enable the tracker to follow the sign more efficiently while maintaining security, the track pursuit drill is used. The drill is a five-step process that will allow the combat tracker to follow the sign quickly and efficiently while maintaining tactical situational awareness. All steps happen almost simultaneously, allowing the tracker to move quickly along the track line.

Step one: Assess the quarry's direction of travel. While following the quarry's track line, the tracker is constantly searching for and identifying the farthest sign left by the quarry. The tracker also evaluates the surrounding terrain to assess all possible routes the quarry may have taken.

Step two: Eliminate all alternate routes. The tracker eliminates any alternate routes possibly taken by the quarry by assessing all openings through vegetation or around obstacles. The tracker rules out those areas where no sign is evident or where any sign discovered is ruled out based on age or other characteristics that don't match the quarry.

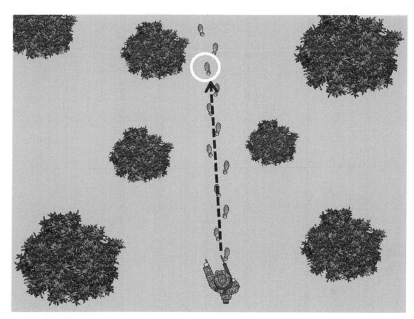

Step one: Assess direction of travel.

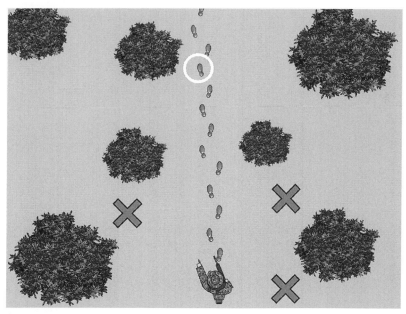

Step two: Eliminate all alternate routes.

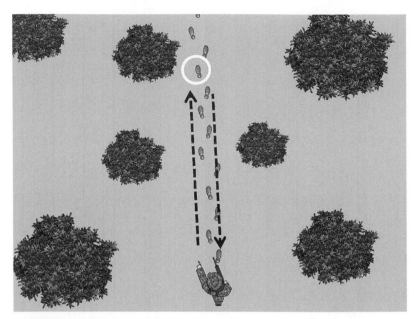

Step three: Connect the farthest sign back to you.

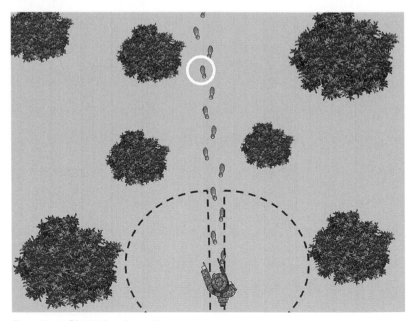

Step four: Check for deception.

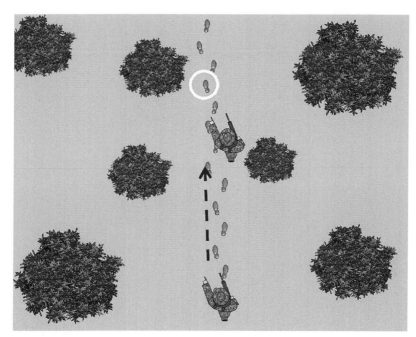

Step five: Patrol forward.

Step three: Visually connect the farthest sign back to your position. The tracker identifies the farthest sign made by the quarry and visually traces the track line back to his position.

Step four: Check for deception. The tracker searches around his position for signs that the quarry may have attempted a counter-tracking technique to conceal a change of direction.

Step five: Patrol forward. The tracker continues to patrol toward the farthest sign identified while scanning and searching the terrain for signs of the enemy.

3

Organization and Tactics

The mission of the combat tracker squad is to gather information in order to reestablish contact or to locate lost or missing friendly personnel. The squad itself should not attempt to make direct contact or become decisively engaged; its goal is to find and fix the enemy so that a finishing force following at a short distance can deploy quickly to destroy him.

Every member of a tracking squad is a combat arms soldier and trained visual tracker capable of performing any tracking duty required during the conduct of a mission. The squad rotates tracking responsibilities between its two teams, always allowing a fresh team to follow the enemy's trail. When conducting a tracking mission, the squad has the capability of locating sign quickly and efficiently at an incident site or when relocating the track line when it's been temporarily lost or has changed direction. Should the squad inadvertently make contact with the enemy, it can provide enough combat power to sustain it until the finishing force deploys forward. The squad should never be split up, which would diminish combat effectiveness and be detrimental to the tracking mission.

DUTY POSITIONS AND RESPONSIBILITIES

Within every military unit, each member has a job to perform in order for the unit to be successful. The combat tracker squad is no exception. Each squad member is responsible for the tasks his position requires, and the success of each individual is dependent on

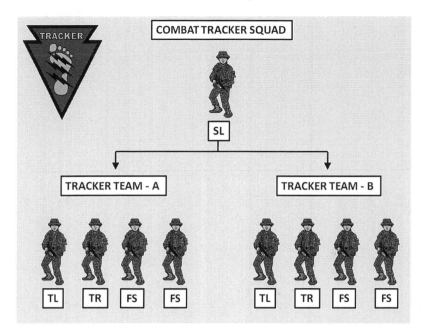

the success of all the others. If one member fails to do his job, the tracking mission and safety of the squad are compromised.

The tracker squad leader is responsible for:

- All the squad does or fails to do
- Planning and conduct of the tracking operation
- Tactical decisions and employment of his squad
- General health and welfare of his squad
- Reporting all relevant information up the chain of command
- Assisting in securing the last known sign
- Planning and conducting collective tracker squad sustainment training
- Accountability of soldiers and equipment
- Submitting the patrol debrief after operations have been concluded

Although the squad leader is a trained and experienced tracker, he does not rotate between tracking and flank security duties. The squad leader is *the* leader of the patrol in command of the tracking mission until contact with the enemy is made and the operation is handed over to the finishing force.

The tracker team leader is responsible for:

- All the team does or fails to do
- Conduct of his team's tracking operation
- Tactical decisions and employment of his team
- General health and welfare of his team
- Reporting all relevant information to the squad leader
- Securing the last known sign
- Providing close-in protection for the tracker as a cover man
- Providing rear security when necessary
- Conducting tracker team sustainment training
- Accountability of soldiers and equipment
- Assisting the squad leader when necessary

Although the team leader is a trained and experienced tracker, he does not perform flank security duties. The team leader may, however, assist the tracker with his tracking responsibilities.

The tracker is responsible for:

- Searching for and following the sign of the quarry
- Reading and interpreting sign
- Communicating all interpretations to the team leader
- Designating the last known sign
- Conducting the lost track drill

Left and right flank security is responsible for:

- Providing flank and frontal security for the tracker and team leader
- Providing early warning of the enemy
- Assisting in conducting the lost track drill
- Identifying track traps
- Locating the track line if it crosses the flanker's path

MOVEMENT FORMATIONS

Squad and team movement formations are used for command control, flexibility, and security. The best formation to use will depend on the mission, terrain, and likelihood of enemy contact. The distance between squad members as well as between teams will depend on terrain, visibility, and the control the squad and team leaders believe is necessary. Leaders should understand that movement formations need to be flexible and should adjust them according to the mission, enemy situation, troops available, terrain, and amount of time and distance between the trackers and the quarry.

TEAM FORMATIONS

A number of formation options are available to the lead tracking team in order to follow the quarry.

V Formation. The V formation is used when the team is moving through open terrain. It offers the leader good control over his

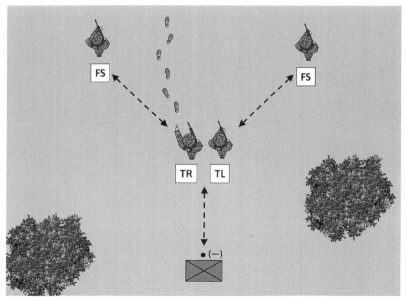

Team V formation

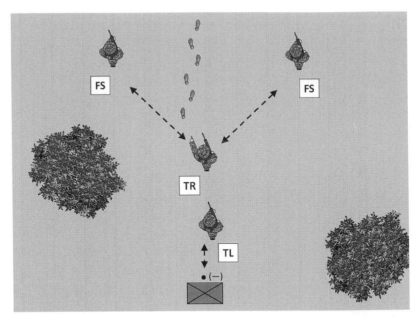

Team Y formation

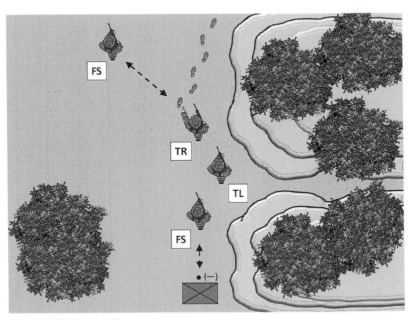

Team half Y formation

team and is flexible, allowing immediate fire in all directions. This formation also offers good all-around local security, particularly for the tracker, when the team leader serves as his cover man.

Y Formation. The Y formation is used in open terrain, is easy to control and flexible, allows immediate fire in all directions, and offers good all-around local security. It provides less security for the tracker, however, by not incorporating a cover man.

Half Y Formation. The half Y formation is used when terrain becomes more restrictive on one side than the other. It is easy to control and flexible.

Modified Wedge Formation. The modified wedge formation (also called the staggered column) is used when terrain becomes restrictive and there is poor visibility between team members, or there are other factors that reduce the leader's control over the team. This formation provides added control necessary when moving through restrictive terrain but offers less security to the front for the tracker.

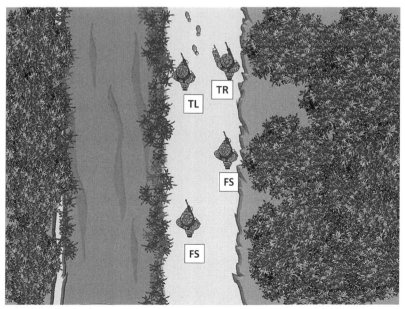

Team modified wedge formation

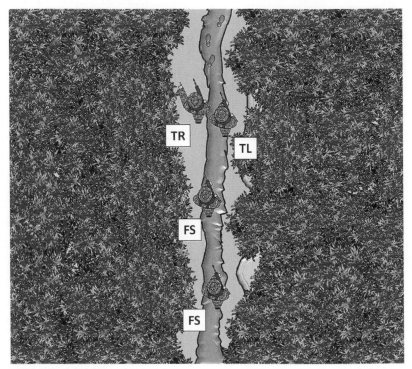

Team file formation

File Formation. The file formation is used when terrain becomes very restrictive and there is poor visibility between team members. It is also easy to control for the team leader but provides less security to the front for the tracker.

Extended Line Formation. The extended line formation is used when the terrain is open and there is little or no vegetation to impede visibility. This formation allows multiple trackers to be used simultaneously and provides increased security to the front if enemy contact is possible. When security permits and terrain is suitable, using this formation can speed up the progress of the pursuit.

Wedge Formation. The wedge formation is used when contact may be imminent. It is flexible and easy to control but does not provide adequate security for the tracker.

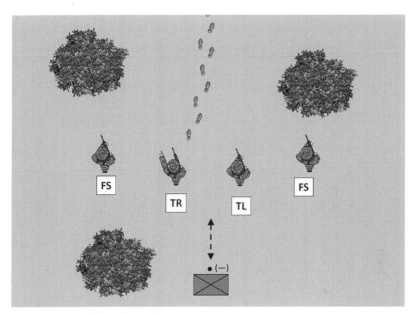

Team extended line formation

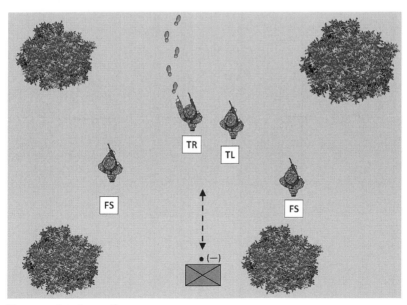

Team wedge formation

SQUAD FORMATIONS

Squad formations describe the relationships between tracker teams within the squad during movement.

Column Formation. The squad column is the formation most used in open terrain. It provides in-depth lateral dispersion without sacrificing control. It offers all-around security and facilitates maneuver. The lead tracker team is the base team if contact is inadvertently made with the enemy. When the squad moves, one of the flank security men in the trail tracker team provides rear security.

Line Formation. The squad line provides maximum security and firepower to the front but little security to the flanks. This formation is best used when a separate element is providing overwatch.

File Formation. The squad file has the same characteristics as the team file. If the squad leader wants to increase control over the formation and be immediately available to make key decisions, he will move forward to the second position from the front. Additional control over the rear of the formation can be provided by moving a team leader to the furthest rear position.

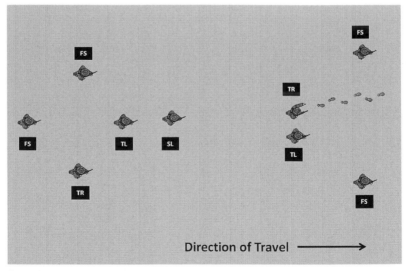

Squad column formation

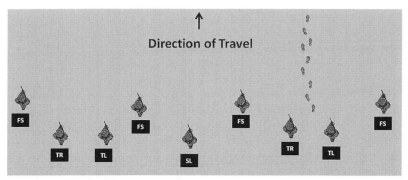

Squad line formation

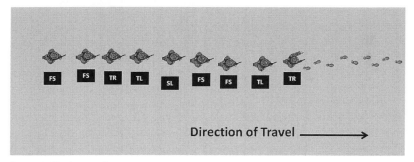

Squad file formation

MOVEMENT TECHNIQUES

Three movement techniques are used by the combat tracker squad: traveling, traveling overwatch, and bounding overwatch. The best technique to use depends on the time and distance between the squad and the quarry as well as the probability of making contact with the enemy. Factors that need to be considered include control, dispersion, speed, and security. Movement techniques, just as with movement formations, are neither fixed nor rigid; they will vary depending on the mission, enemy situation, troops available, terrain, and time and distance between the squad and quarry. Squad members must always maintain visual contact with other squad members, however, and the squad and team leaders control movement with hand and arm signals.

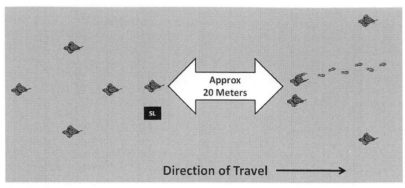

Traveling

Traveling. Traveling is employed when enemy contact is not likely and speed is essential to close the time and distance gap with the quarry. Distance between teams may vary, but 20 meters between teams and 10 meters between individuals is the norm. Traveling provides more control than traveling overwatch but less than bounding overwatch. It also provides minimum dispersion between individuals and teams, offering maximum speed but less security.

Traveling Overwatch. Traveling overwatch is employed when enemy contact is possible. Distance between teams may vary, but 50 meters between teams and 10 to 20 meters between individuals is the norm.

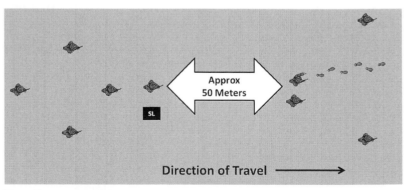

Traveling overwatch

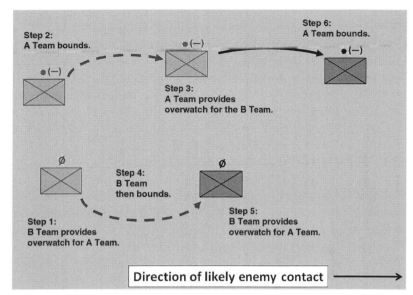

Bounding overwatch

Bounding Overwatch. Bounding overwatch is employed when enemy contact is most likely, as well as when the squad crosses danger areas. The bounding team moves while the other team occupies a position where it can overwatch the bounding team's route. The bounding team must remain within small arms range of the overwatch element at all times. Bounding overwatch offers maximum control, dispersion, and security but minimum speed.

There are two types of bounds that may be employed depending on the situation: Successive bounds are conducted when one team moves to a position, then the overwatching team moves to a position generally in line with the first team. Alternating bounds are conducted when one team moves into a position, then the overwatching team moves to a position forward of the overwatching team but within small arms range. The distance of each bound will depend on terrain, visibility, and the amount of control needed.

Before a bound is made, instructions must be given by the squad leader to his subordinate team leaders. At a minimum, his instructions should include: direction of known enemy location, position of the other team providing overwatch, next overwatch position, route of the team conducting the bound, what to do after the bounding team reaches their next overwatch position, and what to do if enemy contact is made.

HAND AND ARM SIGNALS

Hand and arm signals allow silent communication between patrol members without giving their position away. Using signals can mean the difference between getting compromised and not getting compromised. All hand and arm signals should be known and rehearsed by every member of the patrol. Some signals given here may be different from the standard signals, but they facilitate better communication between squad members.

On Track: Cupped hand with palm facing down

Lost the Track: Cupped hand with palm facing up

Possible Sign: Cupped hand that transitions from palm facing down to palm facing up

Track Trap: Fingers extended and touching, hand closing so that thumb and index finger touch, then releasing to open position

Good: Thumb up

Not Good: Thumb down

Direction of Track Line: Arm extended in direction of track line with fingers extended and touching

Flanker Crossover: Arms extended at shoulder level, rotating inward and crossing over in front of face

Conduct 360: Arm moving in a circle

Enemy: Weapon pointed toward enemy

Halt: Arm bent at the elbow, hand raised, fingers extended and touching

Listen: Hand cupped behind ear

Freeze: Arm bent at elbow, hand raised with fingers closed, making a fist

Danger Area: Arm making a slashing motion across chest

Security: Index and middle finger pointing to the eyes

Patrol Leader: Tugging at collar

Rest Break: Making the motion of breaking a stick

Map Check: Pointing to opposite hand that has palm facing up

Dog Tracker Team: Pointing to nose

LOST TRACK DRILLS

Lost track drills allow the lead tracker team to use different search techniques and procedures to reacquire a track line that has been lost. The drills are systematic exercises that start with individual search procedures conducted by the tracker, progressing to include the entire lead tracker team within the squad if necessary. The drills, if done correctly, will cause little contamination to the search area. (Remember that the more individuals moving around the area searching for sign, the more contamination will occur, and the chance of finding the track quickly lessens). It is extremely important that the team leader plans and controls the lost track drills while maintaining local security.

Trackers should keep in mind that humans are typically lazy and will most likely choose the path of least resistance when selecting a route around an obstacle. These are the "likely avenues" that the tracker will want to focus on when attempting to reacquire the track line.

LAST KNOWN SIGN

The last known sign is always designated by the tracker through hand and arm signals relayed to the team leader, whose job it is to secure the LKS to prevent it from becoming contaminated should the tracker have to conduct a lost track drill. Marking and preserving the LKS allows the tracker a point to return to when attempting to reacquire the track.

The quarry may attempt to employ countertracking techniques to shake off his pursuers. The tracker should know that losing the quarry's sign could be only a matter of taking a few steps in the wrong direction. Although the tracker should never move beyond the last known sign, human error can occur when the tracker thinks he is following the right track but in reality isn't. It is important that the location of the LKS is always well known, marked, guarded, and preserved before any lost track drills are conducted.

INDIVIDUAL LOST TRACK DRILL

The tracker's individual lost track drill is the first step in trying to reacquire a lost track. When the tracker has given the signal that he has lost the sign, the team leader will secure the LKS, and the tracker will begin the individual search procedure.

Step One: Quick Visual Search. While stationary at the LKS, the tracker looks out along the quarry's most likely direction. If no sign is identified the tracker continues the visual search 360 degrees around his position to evaluate all openings in the surrounding terrain and assess all possible routes the quarry may have taken.

If the tracker is standing upright and doesn't observe any sign, he should kneel or squat and try again. Sometimes just changing

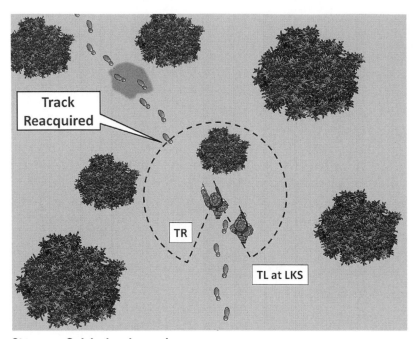

Step one: Quick visual search

the angle at which the track line is viewed will bring out details not observed when standing upright. If the tracker does not reacquire the track, he moves to step two.

Step Two: Tracker Probe. While the team leader secures the LKS, the tracker probes forward to check a disturbance he observed during step one or search likely avenues the quarry may have taken. As the tracker moves forward, he needs to remain conscious of where he's stepped so he doesn't contaminate the area he is searching. If the tracker relocates the sign, he signals to the team leader and the rest of the squad. After reconfirming the sign, the team continues with the pursuit.

If the tracker moves forward and doesn't reacquire the sign, he moves back on his own track line, being careful not to contaminate the ground, and proceeds to step three.

Step Three: Tracker's 360-Degree Search. The tracker's 360-degree search is conducted when steps one and two fail. With the

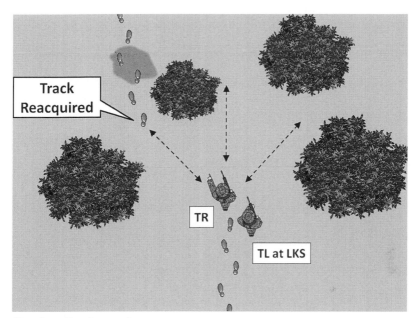

Step two: Tracker probe

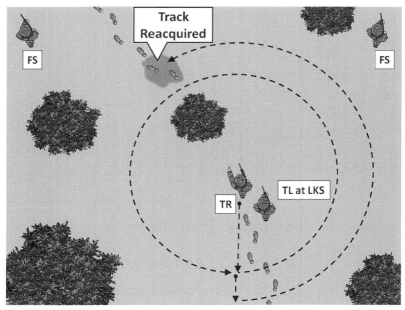

Step three: Tracker's 360-degree search

team leader securing the LKS, the tracker moves back along the track line in case the quarry has walked backwards to deceive the tracker. Once the tracker has moved back a ways from the LKS, he conducts a 360-degree sweep of the area. This sweep is always done within the security of his flankers.

If the tracker relocates the quarry's track line, he signals the team leader, and the team moves forward. After reconfirming the quarry's sign, the squad continues with the operation. If the tracker has not relocated the sign after step three, the team leader may decide to conduct a wider search using a team lost track drill.

TEAM LOST TRACK DRILLS

If individual lost track drills have not reacquired the quarry's track line, the team leader has one flank security member at a time conduct a 360-degree sweep around his position to search for sign in an attempt to reacquire the track line.

Flank Security 360-Degree Searches. When directed by the team leader to conduct a "flanker 360," one flank security member will be directed to move first. The flank security member so designated sweeps his area and a little further than halfway through the center of the V formation (always within observation of the team). If the first flanker does not reacquire the sign, the opposite flanker conducts his 360 sweep when the first flanker returns to his position and the team leader directs him to do so. If the track line is found, the flanker signals to the team leader. The tracker moves forward, and, after confirming the sign, the squad continues with the operation.

Flanker Crossover. When directed by the team leader to conduct a flanker crossover, one flank security member will be directed to move at a time. The right flanker conducts a sweep inside the V formation, moving toward the left flanker's position to search for sign. When he reaches the left flanker's position, he relieves the left flanker and provides security.

The left flanker sweeps the outside area of the formation, searching for sign while moving toward the right flank position. Both

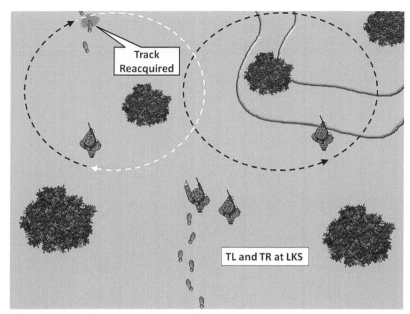

Flank security 360-degree searches

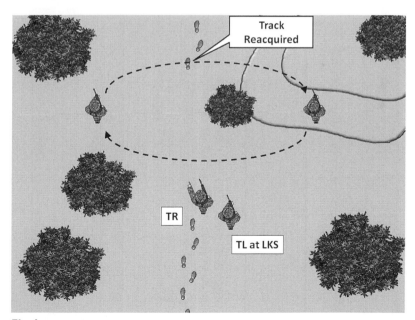

Flanker crossover

flankers must conduct their sweeps within observation of the team. If one of the flankers relocates the quarry's track line, he signals the team leader, and the team continues the operation after the sign is reconfirmed.

Box Search. The box search is used when the lead tracker team is confronted with a large obstacle, danger area, or an area that is heavily contaminated. To use it, the team leader secures the LKS, and the squad leader provides the tracker with a five-point contingency plan along with special instructions. The plan is for those leaving the main body of the patrol; it answers the points of the acronym GOTWA: where the element is *going*, *others* that are going, the *time* they will be gone, *what* to do if they don't return in time, and *actions* by both elements in the event enemy contact is made during separation.

To start a box search, the tracker moves to the flanker's position in the direction the quarry most likely has gone, searching for sign on the way. When the tracker links up with the flanker, he communicates the five-point plan to the flanker. The tracker and flanker box around the obstacle, the tracker looking for sign while the flanker provides security. If the track is reacquired, the team is called up, and the operation continues.

Stream Line Search. The stream line search is used when the team has lost the track near a stream. As with the box search, the team leader secures the LKS and provides the tracker with a five-point contingency plan along with special instructions. The tracker will move to the flanker's position in the direction the quarry most likely has gone, searching for sign on the way. When the tracker links up with the flanker, he communicates the plan, and the tracker and flanker sweep along the stream banks, the tracker looking for sign while the flanker provides security. If the sign is reacquired, the operation continues.

CHANGEOVER PROCEDURE

The tracker cannot track for an indefinite period and must not track when tired. It is critical that, when the tracker hands over his

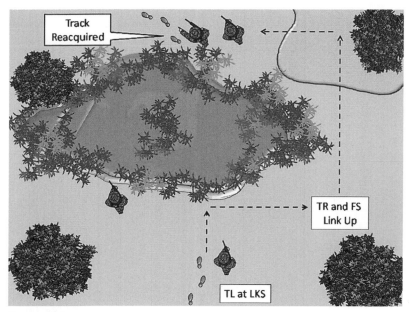

Box search

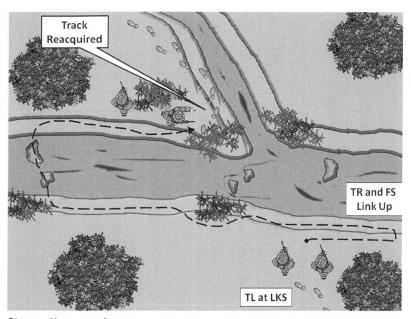

Stream line search

responsibilities to another tracker, the track line is not lost or contaminated and security is maintained.

When the tracker needs a rest or is told to change over by the team leader, the tracker will halt at the last conclusive sign. The team leader provides security while the changeover is conducted. The outgoing tracker briefs the incoming tracker by showing him the sign he is on (which should be conclusive and indicate the farthest sign) and updating him on the quarry's track picture.

If the incoming tracker is satisfied that he has acquired the quarry's sign, he takes over. If he is not, the first tracker continues along the track until the next conclusive sign. The changeover procedure is then repeated until the incoming tracker is confident he is on track. The incoming tracker reconfirms all information communicated by the outgoing tracker, who then takes over one of the flanker's duties. When the flanker position is assumed, the new tracker continues as lead tracker.

CROSSING DANGER AREAS

The combat tracker squad is extremely vulnerable when crossing danger areas, of which there are two types: linear danger areas and open danger areas. Examples of danger areas are open fields, roads, trails, urban terrain, and natural or man-made obstacles, such as boulders or bridges. If the enemy is aware he is being tracked, he may attempt to ambush the squad at one of these points. In order to cross a danger area safely while still tracking the quarry, the squad must move deliberately so the area is not contaminated.

LINEAR DANGER AREAS

Linear danger areas are locations where a patrol is vulnerable to enemy observation or fire predominately from the flanks: examples include roads, trails, and streams. When the first member of the squad to detect a linear danger area indicates the obstacle by hand

and arm signal, the squad stops, kneels, and conducts a security halt: stopping, looking, listening, and smelling for indicators of the enemy. The tracker and his cover man (the team leader) then cautiously track forward to the near side of the danger area where the sign enters the danger area. Without exposing themselves, they provide security up and down the danger area and protect the last known sign.

The squad leader and two members from the trail tracker team move up to the tracker and cover man's position. The squad leader controls the crossing point, and the two squad members from the trail team relieve the tracker and cover man by providing near-side security up and down the linear danger area.

The tracker and cover man continue to track the sign across the danger area, ensuring that they confirm the exit point. They then move, remaining on sign, to the limit of visibility on the far side of the danger area; then they halt.

The two squad members from the rear tracker team continue to provide security up and down the danger area until the entire squad crosses. Upon reaching the exit point on the far side of the danger area, the tracker and team leader from the trail team stop to provide security so the two flankers on the near side can cross. Finally, when the entire squad has crossed, the squad leader gives the order to continue tracking.

OPEN DANGER AREAS

When crossing large or small open danger areas, the squad conducts a bounding overwatch. The first member of the squad to detect the danger area indicates the obstacle to the rest of the squad, which conducts a security halt. The tracker and his cover man then cautiously track forward to the near side of the danger area.

The squad and trail team leaders move up to the lead tracker and team leader's position to survey the danger area. The squad leader designates an overwatch position for the trail team to occupy and issues a contingency plan to the trail team leader.

The trail team leader moves back to his team, disseminates the plan to the rest of his team, and then moves to the overwatch position designated by the squad leader, remaining in this position until told to move. When the overwatch element is in position, the lead tracker team and squad leader continue to track across the danger area—never moving out of effective small-arms range of the overwatch element. Depending on the size of the danger area, the crossing may take one or more bounds.

SECURITY HALTS

To conduct a security halt, the squad stops and kneels, facing out to ensure that security is provided a full 360 degrees around the squad. The tracker then signals, marks the last known sign, and backtracks several meters before breaking off the track. The LNS remains outside the security perimeter. This is to ensure that the last known sign will not get contaminated if members move around the security perimeter. At the end of the halt, the tracker moves up and reacquires the last known sign in order to continue the pursuit.

PATROL BASE PROCEDURES

If the combat tracker squad has to "sleep on the track," it may need to occupy a patrol base from sometime before last light until sometime after first light. Occupation of the patrol base is conducted in the same way as a halt. The squad leader must ensure that the last known sign has been clearly marked and recorded. The squad moves to a location not too far from the last known sign to prevent members from contaminating the track line during the night. The squad then places claymore mines as required and conducts stand-to from fifteen minutes before last light until fifteen minutes after last light. Then it establishes a security and alert plan, conducts patrol base activities such as equipment maintenance, eats, and rests. During the night, the squad must maintain noise and light discipline.

During patrol base activities, the squad leader also debriefs the squad as to the track picture over the last twenty-four hours. Prior to stand-to, all equipment is packed. Stand-to is conducted from fifteen minutes before first light until fifteen minutes after first light. Upon completion, the claymore mines are recovered. The combat tracker squad then conducts a meal plan and establishes radio contact with the TCE. After the meal and communications check, the tracker leads the squad back to the last known sign to continue the pursuit.

IMMEDIATE ACTION DRILLS

Immediate action drills (IADs) are individual and collective actions rapidly executed without a deliberate decision-making process. They are executed in situations that involve enemy contact. The drills are simple, well-rehearsed courses of action in which all squad members are trained so that a minimum of signals or commands are required.

Visual or physical enemy contacts are usually unexpected, at close range, and short in duration (especially in counterinsurgency operations). Effective fire, or the threat of effective fire, often provides leaders little or no time to fully estimate the enemy situation and issue orders. In these situations, IADs provide a way to swiftly initiate positive offensive or defensive action, as appropriate. They should be well rehearsed before the conduct of any mission. Examples of IADs include contact front, contact left/right, contact rear, attack, break contact, near ambush, far ambush, react to sniper, and react to indirect.

The mission of the combat tracker team is to find, fix, and finish the enemy. When conducting a pursuit operation, the combat tracker squad finds and fixes the enemy, and the tracker support group typically finishes him. In reality, however, the combat tracker squad will often be the first element that makes enemy contact.

IF THE ENEMY IS OBSERVED OR HIS LOCATION IDENTIFIED

The enemy's position could be identified in a number of ways; it might have been seen, heard, or even smelled. If the enemy has been detected without his knowledge, the squad conducts a halt and provides security in the direction of the enemy. The tracker support group then moves up and takes over the operation before conducting an attack on the enemy.

The tracker squad may not have any indication that it closed the time-distance gap with the enemy, however, and so find itself in a chance contact. It is critical when the squad is following a warm or hot track that the support group be as close as possible without giving away the trackers' position—close enough so that it can manuever and close with the enemy quickly should contact occur.

In the event of chance contact, the combat tracker squad should move to a defendable position, laying down suppressive fire for the tracker support group as they make their way forward to maneuver on the enemy. Depending on the situation the combat tracker squad may need to radio for close air or indirect fire support.

ACTIONS TAKEN AFTER ENEMY CONTACT

Upon completion of the assault, the tracker squad and support group conduct consolidation and reorganization, which include clearing the area of the enemy, establishing a limit of advance, and preparing and sending a situation report. If it's safe to do so, the tracker and a flanker conduct a 360-degree search to look for sign of enemy escape routes. The squad and support group will also make a plan to conduct a pursuit after the tracker and flanker have returned with the results of their search. If all enemy personnel have not been accounted for, the operation resumes.

Rally Points. If the squad was required to break contact under pressure, the tracker squad will have to move back to a position to consolidate and reorganize. Rally points provide a location for squad members to reassemble and reorganize if they become dispersed. Everyone within the squad must know which rally point to move to at each phase of the patrol should they become separated from the unit. They must also know what actions are required when occupying a rally point and how long they should wait before moving to another rally point.

Rally points should be easily identifiable during both daylight and limited visibility, show no signs of recent enemy activity, offer cover and concealment, be defendable for short periods of time, and be located away from natural lines of drift and high-speed avenues of approach.

En route rally points are designated approximately every 100 to 400 meters (based on terrain, vegetation, and visibility). When the squad leader designates a new en route rally point, the previously designated one goes into effect. This prevents uncertainty about which point squad members should move to if enemy contact occurs immediately after a new rally point is designated.

There are three ways to designate a rally point: physically occupying the rally point for a short period of time, passing by at a distance and designating it using arm-and-hand signals, or walking through it and designating it using arm-and-hand signals.

Actions conducted at the rally point include:

- Conducting stop, look, listen, and smell (SLLS)
- Pinpointing the squad's current location
- Contacting the higher command of tracker support group
- Issuing a fragmentary order to the current mission, if needed
- Preparing for the continuation of the mission
- Accounting for personnel and equipment
- Reestablishing the chain of command, if necessary
- Disseminating important information among squad members

Challenge and Password. Should the combat tracker squad become dispersed and need to occupy a rally point or patrol base or link up with another element, the squad will want to determine whether the element making contact is a friend or an enemy.

Challenge and passwords are used to do this. Units conducting operations "outside the wire" of friendly bases use two methods of challenging and receiving a password.

In the *odd number system,* the leader specifies an odd number to be used. The challenge can be any number less than the specified number. The password will be the number that must be added to it to equal the specified number.

In the *running password system,* a code word alerts a unit that friendly soldiers are approaching in a less-than-organized manner and possibly under pressure. The code word is followed by the number of soldiers approaching (Guinness 7, for example). This prevents the enemy from penetrating a friendly group.

TARGET INDICATORS

When patrolling, the combat tracker squad is not only following the tracks of the quarry but also searching for the enemy himself. Seven different target indicators will help the tracker detect the enemy when he is close.

All *shapes* within nature are irregular. Military equipment and personnel are easily recognizable by their regular geometric shape and outline.

Shadows occur where light cannot reach because it is blocked by an object. Shadows—cast by the sun or moon—will create a "copy" of an object and give away its presence. An object concealed within shadow is more difficult to detect since the object will not cast a shadow. When the sun or moon moves, however, so does the shadow, and a previously hidden object may become visible. Remember that shadows contained within a confined space are normally darker than other shadows and can attract attention.

A *silhouette* is an object's outline and featureless interior, with the silhouetted object usually being dark. The enemy may be silhouetted against a contrasting background, exposing his position.

Surface is indicated by texture or shine. If the color and texture of the surface of an object contrasts with its surroundings, it will be noticeable. Areas of flattening or disturbance will be identified because their surface is different from the ground around them.

Spacing is how like objects are positioned relative to each other. Natural objects are rarely, if ever, regularly spaced. Regular spacing draws attention.

Color causes objects to be more obvious against a background of a contrasting color: a dark object against a light background, or a light object against a dark background.

The human eye is attracted to *movement.* A motionless object may be hard to detect. A slow-moving object may be detected more easily than one that is stationary; sudden, jerky movements will attract the human eye quickly.

REFLEXIVE SHOOTING

An enemy attempting to hide from pursuers will often wait until he is inevitably going to be discovered before opening fire at close range. Soldiers in the tracker squad need to react quickly and efficiently to eliminate the enemy before the enemy eliminates them.

Trackers should be aware of the "combat engagement ring" and will respond in different ways to engagements that occur at close range (within 25 meters) and those that occur at long range (beyond 25 meters). Close-range engagements require speed over precision. Long-range engagements require accuracy over speed (the use of a "slow aimed fire" technique is the preferred method).

While patrolling, the tracker positions his rifle butt firmly in the pocket of his shoulder with the barrel pointed down at a 45-degree angle so the sights can be brought into position quickly. In extremely dangerous situations, when the enemy may be near, the lead team of the squad advances with weapons shouldered, scanning and aiming as they advance.

TYPES OF REFLEXIVE SHOOTING

One of three quick engagement techniques is used when an enemy suddenly appears.

Rapid Aimed Fire. This technique uses an imperfect sight picture—when the front sight post is in line with the target, the shooter squeezes the trigger. Rapid aimed fire is used against targets out to 15 meters; it is fairly accurate and very fast.

Aimed Quick Kill. This technique involves using a good spot weld and placing the front sight post flush on top of the rear peep sight. It is used for very quick shots out to 12 meters. This technique is the fastest and most accurate.

Instinctive Fire. This technique is used when the immediate domination of the engagement is critical. The shooter focuses on the target and points the weapon in the target's general direction, using muscle memory to compensate for lack of aim. This technique should be used only in emergencies and should be followed up rapidly with aimed shots.

When suddenly confronted with an enemy at close range, the tracker must react aggressively. Rapidly aimed semiautomatic fire is the most effective method of engaging the enemy. When each round is fired, the weapon's recoil makes the front sight post move. Do not fight the recoil. Allow the weapon to recoil naturally and immediately reacquire the target with the front sight and follow up with another round to the enemy.

The enemy must be eliminated immediately. Shots that wound and do not incapacitate the enemy are better than misses but may allow the enemy to return fire. Firing two shots in combination is known as firing a controlled pair. The tracker aggressively continues to maneuver on his enemy while firing controlled pairs until the threat is eliminated. The tracker needs to achieve solid, well-placed shots to the chest and head. Upon eliminating the enemy, the tracker scans to ensure that no other threats exist before he lowers his weapon.

COVER SHOOT TECHNIQUE

The goal of the cover shoot is to locate an enemy's position and kill him without actually seeing him. The cover shoot does not involve

Cover shoot technique

randomly spraying bullets in the enemy's direction but is a deliberate and methodical drill designed to have the greatest effect while expending the least amount of ammo possible.

When the combat tracker squad makes enemy contact, the objective is for each soldier to fire within his individual sector, overlapping with members to his left and right. Enemy locations are engaged from left to right in the direction of enemy contact; the nearest enemy position is engaged first before moving further out and away.

When firing into an area that features trees or rocks or any object that can provide cover, the soldier fires one or two rounds in rapid succession close to the ground immediately in front of the enemy's suspected position and to the left side of the solid object. (Most people are right-handed and will use cover to protect themselves; therefore, when engaging the enemy, the soldier shoots at the left side of the object as he is looking at it).

When conducting this drill, squad members shoot directly into and through the enemy's position, keeping their aim low—the first round is intended to "skip" and strike a prone target. Each round is fired in a deliberately aimed and controlled manner. These actions are repeated to the right of the cover—one or two rounds. The soldier then moves his aim to the next area of cover and repeats the process.

STEPS TO ENGAGE A HIDDEN ENEMY

When making enemy contact, depending on the situation, the lead tracker team or the entire squad may deploy on line, facing in the direction of the enemy. Each soldier splits his target area into sectors to ensure overlapping fields of fire with his other squad members—this is typically the ten o'clock to two o'clock position to the tracker's front.

After engaging positions of likely cover, the soldier places one aimed shot into a 12-by-12-inch area at ground level to the left of the cover. Shot placement is from front to rear and rear to front of each sector. The soldier waits momentarily, and if there is no movement, he places another well-aimed shot at ground level in a 12-by-12-inch area to the right side of the cover. If there is movement on the left side of the cover, the soldier is in position to immediately fire another round into the same area. If there is no movement, the soldier seeks another position of likely cover.

The squad must ensure an even distribution of fire. When the soldier has accurately engaged all positions of likely cover within his sector, he will cease fire and wait for guidance from the team or squad leader.

4

Operational Employment

"Reconnaissance units must locate insurgent forces, tracks, or other indicators of direction or location. In rural and some border operations, well-trained Trackers can identify and follow insurgent tracks that are hours or even days old. Units tracking the insurgent must be prepared to react to insurgent contact and avoid likely ambush situations. Leaders must ensure support for the reconnaissance force if it is compromised."
—*Field Manual M 3-24.2,*
"Tactics in Counterinsurgency"

The combat tracking mission will complement a full spectrum of military operations; it is a focused, collective effort conducted with two or more combat tracker units in support of larger operations. Combat tracking relies primarily on the human dynamic instead of technical means. It supports offensive operations—such as movement to contact, attack, exploitation, and pursuit—and defensive operations, through reconnaissance missions to develop the enemy situation forward of friendly units' defensive lines.

It also supports security operations, such as screening and area and local operations that provide early and accurate warning of enemy operations, allowing friendly forces time and space to react. As well, it supports reconnaissance operations, such as route, zone, and area reconnaissance, and reconnaissance-in-force operations that provide critical information to aid units in their intelligence

preparation of the battlefield process.

Finally, the combat tracking mission supports combat search-and-rescue operations, locating and recovering lost or missing friendly personnel by identifying the personnel's position and permitting recovery.

OBJECTIVES OF A COMBAT TRACKING OPERATION

The objectives of a combat tracking operation are to find, fix, finish, exploit, analyze, and disseminate.

FIND

The tracker squad finds the quarry by tracking his "patterns of life." While the quarry moves from point to point, the squad follows the string of physical evidence along the track line and notes the direction traveled, evidence found, and locations visited. Connections between the evidence, locations, and direction are made, and the quarry's life pattern emerges. Employing multiple combat tracker squads allows one squad to follow the quarry's track line while one or more squads leapfrog ahead along the direction of travel to track traps in the expected path. At the traps, one or more squads will search for enemy sign. If it is found, the team that finds it will continue the pursuit; the squad that began the tracking operation will be called off and will become the bounding element. Employing these techniques allows the pursuit force to cut time and distance between it and the quarry. If the quarry knows he is being pursued, this technique will also create mental and physical pressure, which often leads to mistakes.

FIX

The combat tracker squad fixes the quarry's position by continuously collecting material that creates an accurate track picture.

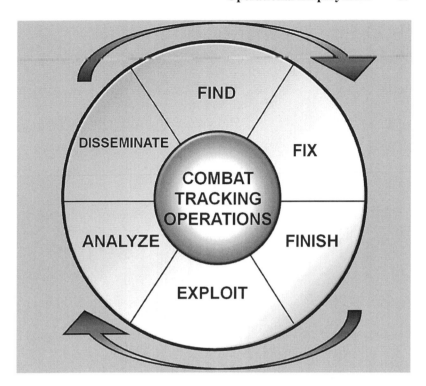

The information will reveal rest stops, camp locations, caches, surveillance positions, entry and exit routes, villages visited, and so on. It will also provide possible links to enemy elements operating nearby. As details about the quarry are filled in, the squad can anticipate where the quarry is most likely to travel or spend time.

As the gap between the tracker squad and quarry is narrowed, and the sign becomes fresher, the squad takes great care to not give away its position. When the squad locates the quarry without being compromised, it provides observation until the support group can maneuver. If the tracker squad makes contact with an enemy, the squad leader immediately calls the support group so it can quickly deploy. (If the enemy force is smaller than the tracking squad, however, it may be prudent for the squad to eliminate the enemy threat itself.)

FINISH

The window of opportunity to engage and destroy an enemy is usually small; making the most of it requires a well-rehearsed procedure to transfer the operation from the tracker squad to the support group or finishing force. Rarely is there time to create an elaborate plan. Instead, the squad must adapt a known drill to the existing combat situation and rapidly execute it. The tracker squad and support group also must be prepared to conduct follow-on operations based on what occurs during contact, or on information collected from exploitation of the objective.

EXPLOIT

Once the objective is secured, the squad and support group exploit it for enemy information. The tracker team conducts a 360-degree search around the perimeter of the objective to determine the enemy's exit route. If the exit route is found, the squad may continue the pursuit.

Exploitation of the objective should be methodical and detailed. Collecting potential intelligence requires well-rehearsed search procedures as well as a plan to question enemy detainees tactically. Information gained will feed the intelligence operations cycle. Enemy documents and pocket litter as well as information obtained from questioning may further reveal the enemy's capabilities, locations, and intentions.

ANALYZE

Some enemy impression evidence and collected information may be immediately actionable so the pursuit can continue. Other information may be of use for future operations after it has been corroborated.

DISSEMINATE

Information disseminated to commanders and other units conducting operations will ensure that everyone knows everything the combat tracker squad knows. Even if information appears to be irrelevant, it still is reported, because it just may be the key that unlocks the door for someone else.

COMBAT TRACKER MISSIONS

There are four types of combat tracker missions. *Pursuit missions* are undertaken to make or reestablish contact with an enemy who is fleeing from an incident site where an attack or sighting has occurred. Combat tracker squad employment in pursuit missions is divided into two categories, preplanned and reactive employment. In the first, the squad should be employed for immediate follow-on/exploitation purposes for the following operations: deliberate attack, ambush, movement to contact, cordon and search, defense, and any combat patrol task.

In the second, a squad should always be available as part of a quick reaction force to react to situations as they occur. The squad would normally deploy in order to pursue the enemy when an enemy contact has occurred, a sighting of the enemy has been reported and needs to be investigated, or recently obtained intelligence information has made it necessary to employ the squad.

Reconnaissance missions are undertaken to trail or surveil the enemy to acquire and report information on enemy locations, routes, or areas of support or to backtrack to gain information about where the enemy came from, which may lead to cache sites, safe houses, camps, or areas that provide enemy refuge and support. In this task, the squad's role is to search for enemy sign in likely areas of enemy movement and, if sign is found, to follow it to gather as much information as possible.

There are many reasons why a combat tracker squad could be employed for reconnaissance tasks: to locate and report on signs of the enemy in areas not covered by normal patrolling, to investigate intelligence information or sightings of the enemy, to recon areas where enemy activity is expected, or to gain information on enemy tactics at an incident site.

The third category of missions, *security missions,* are missions undertaken to safeguard the force through the conduct of perimeter patrols, route clearing, and security patrols to counter hostile surveillance.

Finally, *personnel recovery missions* are missions undertaken to recover lost or missing friendly personnel.

FUNDAMENTALS OF
COMBAT TRACKING OPERATIONS

For combat tracking operations to be successful, four fundamentals must be applied. Information collected by the combat tracker squad must be *reported accurately and quickly,* then disseminated to other elements on the ground involved in the pursuit. Combat tracker assets must acquire and report accurate information on the enemy in a timely manner. Enemy information, whether positive or negative, that is not reported immediately and quickly exploited may lose value and contribute to the enemy's ability to evade pursuers.

Combat tracking units must *retain freedom of movement*—meaning they must have the ability to move wherever the sign takes them—to successfully complete their missions. The squad does not have the luxury of choosing its route; it must go where the track line takes it.

A tracker squad must also *gain and maintain enemy contact.* Contact can range from surveillance to close combat. Once the tracker squad makes contact with the enemy, it maintains contact unless directed otherwise or if the survival of the squad is at risk. Surveillance, combined with stealth, is often sufficient to maintain contact and is the preferred method to use until the support group is able to eliminate the enemy.

Finally, the unit must *develop the situation rapidly* to determine the enemy's composition, dispositions, activities, and movements and assess the potential implications of that information.

REPORTING INFORMATION

Before transmitting a message, a soldier must first *listen* to avoid interfering with another transmission. Transmissions need to contain clear, complete, and concise messages. A soldier making a transmission must speak clearly and slowly, in natural phrases, enunciating each word. This will provide the receiver of the message time to write the message down if need be.

The use of brevity codes and prowords will help keep communications short. Some principles to keep in mind when communicating information over the radio are contained in the acronym RSVP.

- Rhythm: The pattern formed by stressed and unstressed syllables. Keeping a smooth, natural rhythm will make your words more understandable.
- Speed: The rate at which the message is communicated. Speak slower than you would in normal conversation.
- Volume: The loudness of the voice. Speak only as loud as you would in normal conversaton; shouting will only cause distortion.
- Pitch: The degree of inflection in the voice. Keep the pitch of your voice steady and slightly higher than usual; higher-pitched voices transmit better.

When communicating grid coordinates, remember that the listener will most likely be writing the coordinates down. It is important that you adjust your rhythm and speed and repeat the grids twice. For example, for a six-digit grid, you should say: "1, 2 . . . 3 [break] 4, 5 . . . 6. I say again, 1, 2 . . . 3 [break] 4, 5 . . . 6." For an eight-digit grid, you should say: "1, 2, 3 . . . 4 [break] 5, 6, 7 . . . 8. I say again, 1, 2, 3 . . . 4 [break] 5, 6, 7 . . . 8."

TRACKER NINE-LINE SITUATION REPORT

The "tracker nine-line" is first given to the tracker control element when the squad is ready to commence a pursuit and again every time the quarry's direction changes or when new information becomes available. The nine-line is important not only because it notifies the higher command of information about the quarry but also because it provides information for the control element to track the squad's progress and coordinate with other units operating in the area.

Line 1: LOCATION	Grid: 12S PJ 1,2 . . . 3,4,5 . . . 6
Line 2: NUMBER	Two enemy all male
Line 3: DIRECTION OF MOVEMENT	Northeast [use only cardinal directions such as north, south, northwest, and so on]
Line 4: AGE OF THE TRACK	Six hours [this is the best guess]
Line 5: TRACK DESCRIPTION	One lug-and-star-type Vibram sole boot Alpha: twelve inches Bravo: four and a half inches Charlie: four inches Delta: three and three quarters of an inch One flat, running-type shoe in a Z-style zigzag pattern Alpha: thirteen inches Bravo: five inches Charlie: four and a half inches Delta: four and one quarter of an inch
Line 6: SPEED AND LOAD CARRIED	Walking pace, stride is thirty inches, stride width six inches, quarry appears to be carrying weight
Line 7: TACTICS BEING EMPLOYED	Quarry is not attempting to conduct any countertracking techniques
Line 8: WEAPONS EMPLOYED	One of the quarry appears to be armed with an AK-type rifle, and one of the quarry may be armed with an RPG-7
Line 9: ADDITIONAL INFORMATION	Two Camel cigarettes butts and one empty water bottle were found where the quarry rested

After the initial tracker nine-line is communicated to the control element, every nine-line that follows is communicated line by line with just the changes. For example, if a change needs to be reported to line 1 only, the squad leader would report:

CTS	TCE
T06 this is T11 over	T11 this is T06 over
T06 this is T11 prepare to copy tracker nine-line over	Roger T11 this is T06 send tracker nine-line over
T06 Line 1 . . . Grid: 12S . . . PJ . . . 12 . . . 6, 45 . . . 8 . . . Line 2 through 9 . . . No change over	Roger T11 I copy . . . Line 1 . . . Grid: 12S . . . PJ . . . 12 . . . 6, 45 . . . 8 . . . Line 2 through 9 . . . No change over
Roger T11 . . . T06 out	

SALUTE REPORT
The SALUTE report is one type of report that provides basic who, what, where, and when information about the enemy.

SIZE:	Seven enemy personnel (personnel or vehicles)
ACTIVITY:	Traveling northeast
LOCATION:	12R GW 123 456
UNIT/UNIFORM:	Tan shirts, woodland BDU-type bottoms, 3 wearing sandals, 4 wearing black boots, all have AK chest harnesses, 2 have packs
TIME:	202100RJAN2011
EQUIPMENT:	One RPK machine gun, one RPG-7, and five AKM rifles

REPORTING A PERSON OF INTEREST
This type of report aids in the description of an individual.

A Age:	Bracket the person's age, i.e. 25–30
B Build:	Thin, athletic, fat, and so on

C	Clothing top to bottom:	White shirt, black pants, white tennis shoes
D	Distinguishing features:	Scars or tattoos, i.e. diagonal scar over left eye
E	Eyes:	Color, shape: oval, brown
F	Face:	Round, pointy, square, and so on; black hair
G	Gait:	Hunched, fast, and so on; tall and upright
H	Height:	Bracket, i.e. 5.8'–6.0'

REPORTING WEAPONS

The acronym TACS aids in the description of weapons.

T	Type:	Medium or light machine gun, rifle, shotgun, or pistol
A	Ammo:	Belt, magazine, and so on
C	Carriage:	Back of truck, holstered, carried, slung over shoulder
S	Sights:	Iron, scope

REPORTING VEHICLES

The acronym SCRIM aids in the description of vehicles.

S	Shape:	4 by 4, truck, sedan, hatchback, jeep, convertible, and so on
C	Color:	Blue, white, red, and so on
R	Registration:	[if observed] TRM 285
I	Identifying features:	Hard top, soft top, bumper stickers, roof racks, dent on left panel, and so on
M	Make and Model:	Ford Ranger

REPORTING IMPRESSIONS

One way of reporting foot impressions over the radio is to build a footwear impression data book of common footwear soles worn in the area of operations. This will aid in the communication of impression characteristics when reporting. When the squad leader reports line 5 of the tracker nine-line, he can simply cross-reference the quarry's sole pattern and report "Delta four" then provide the

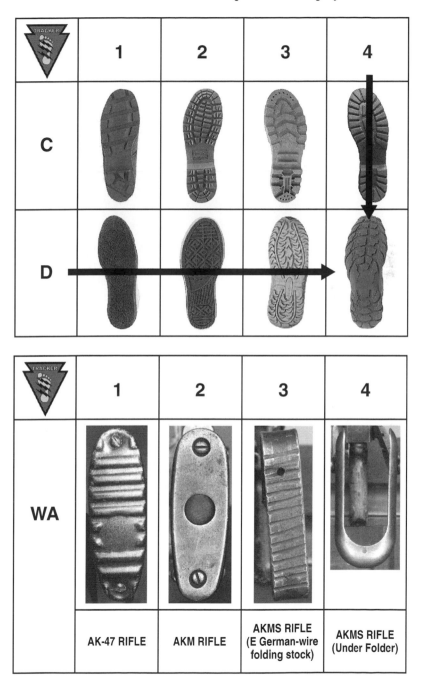

TRACKER	1	2	3	4
C				
D				

TRACKER	1	2	3	4
WA	AK-47 RIFLE	AKM RIFLE	AKMS RIFLE (E German-wire folding stock)	AKMS RIFLE (Under Folder)

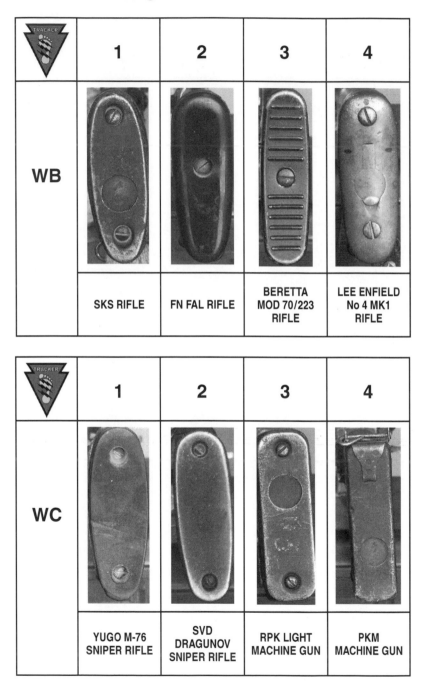

TRACKER	1	2	3	4
WB	SKS RIFLE	FN FAL RIFLE	BERETTA MOD 70/223 RIFLE	LEE ENFIELD No 4 MK1 RIFLE

TRACKER	1	2	3	4
WC	YUGO M-76 SNIPER RIFLE	SVD DRAGUNOV SNIPER RIFLE	RPK LIGHT MACHINE GUN	PKM MACHINE GUN

	1	2
WD	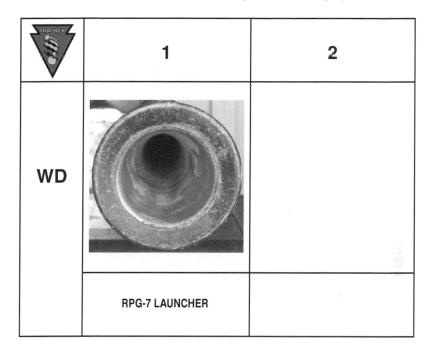	
	RPG-7 LAUNCHER	

A, B, C, and D measurements. Weapon and vehicle impressions can be reported over the radio in the same way.

THE TRACKER CONTROL ELEMENT

The tracker control element's primary responsibility is to support combat tracker squads in the field, coordinate and track the employment of multiple squads during the conduct of an operation, and relay time-sensitive information concerning the enemy. Each squad reports back to the TCE, who is typically colocated with the higher unit's tactical operations center. Tracker squads stay in contact with the TCE through periodic nine-lines sent by radio. These provide real-time information for the TCE.

The TCE needs to have a complete understanding of how the combat tracker squads operate and so should be a trained and experienced tracker himself. This enables him to better support units in the field by anticipating needs and understanding problems that may occur and how to overcome them. The TCE will be required

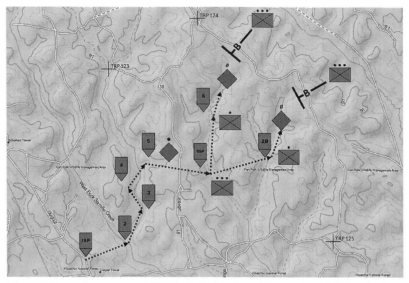

The TCE's primary responsibility is to track and support multiple combat tracking squads during an operation.

to brief the command and handle questions as well as deal with the propensity for commanders and staff to micromanage the operation. Commanders must realize that the squad is not just following tracks, it is following an enemy, who is unpredictable.

The tracker control element's responsibilities include:

- Providing recommendations and advice to the commander on the capabilities and employment of squads
- Maintaining constant communication with the squads when they are deployed
- Maintaining a situation map and annotating the progress of the tracking operation
- Maintaining a chronological record on a daily staff journal or duty officer's log (DA Form 1594) of reports and messages that have been received and transmitted of all important events that have occurred as well as the actions taken in response to those actions. (The journal covers a twenty-four-hour period.)

- Alerting and deploying reserve tracker squads when necessary
- Controlling multiple squads when employed
- Rotating tracker squads when necessary
- Planning and coordinating resupply to the squads when required
- Conducting adjacent unit coordinations when a combat tracker squad approaches a friendly unit's area of responsibility
- Continually monitoring and tracking the squad's movement while assessing the direction of the quarry and coordinating the employment of blocking forces or artillery or air support
- Preventing squads from being used for inappropriate missions and protecting them from commanders and staff who may attempt to interfere with the conduct of the operation

DEPLOYMENT

If more than one squad is allocated, it's possible that two combat tracker squads may be on immediate standby twenty-four hours a day. When the teams are alerted, they should be deployed to the incident site by the quickest means available—typically rotary-wing aircraft. If air support is not available, however, the squads may have to convoy to the incident site.

An example of how tracker squads may be deployed is given here: The ready squad is alerted and called up for operational duty. *When* the squad is first notified for employment information collected and reported is often critical to conducting operations. The information reported must be accurate, current, and relevant. If such information is given to the squad before it hits the ground it will speed up coordination. Time is always a factor—the chances of interdicting the enemy after contact occurs decrease as time passes.

The squad leader is briefed on what happened, where the incident took place (where the squad is going), method of infiltration, whom to contact and conduct coordinations with once on the ground, what call signs and frequencies will be used, what friendly forces are operating in the area, and who the tracker support group will be.

Several factors will influence the timeliness of deployment, including the information reported and disseminated to the tracker unit, the availability of aircraft as well as other supporting assets, the current and forecasted weather conditions, the time of day, the nature of the terrain, and the time delay from when the incident occurred to when the tracker unit was notified.

If available, a second standby squad is alerted to a one-hour notice of movement. If a second squad is required and alerted, it will be employed to conduct a new mission if the enemy splits up or to assist the first squad by deploying well ahead of it, along the quarry's direction of movement, to search for the quarry's track line and close the time-distance gap between the unit in pursuit and the quarry. It will also take over if necessary for the squad already conducting the tracking operation and stand by to be alerted for a new mission, if one should arise.

EXPLOITATION OF AN INCIDENT SITE

When the tracker squad arrives at the incident site, the situation may be chaotic, especially after an IED incident. A checklist of tasks will help the unit coordinate and exploit the site.

1. Establish security if the site has not already been secured.
2. Do not enter the site immediately. First scan and appraise the incident site prior to entering and investigating. You do not want to contaminate the enemy's sign. Determine the best method of conducting the investigation and approach the incident site cautiously, ensuring further contamination does not occur.
3. Identify the on-ground commander (if there is one) and conduct coordinations on the current situation (friendly and enemy), information known about the quarry, the limit of friendly advance, and the available tracker support group.
4. Do not hinder explosive ordnance detachment or weapons intelligence teams that are conducting an investigation at an IED site.

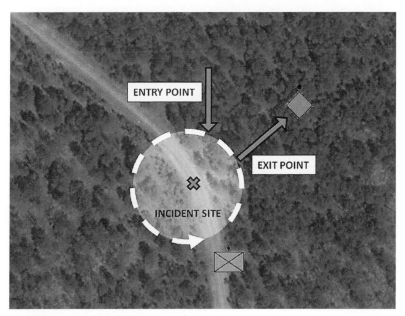

Exploitation of an incident site. Either the entry route, or the exit route, or both, may be exploited.

5. Confirm and record the squad's current grid location on a map.

6. Assign tasks to squad members (photographer, recorder, sketcher, and so on) to expedite the exploitation process.

7. Locate the quarry's tracks and other forensic evidence by conducting a 360-degree search (employing the left and right flank security to conduct the search if tactically feasible) around and well outside the incident site, staying clear of areas that have already been contaminated. Locate, mark, and report to the squad leader any sign indicating entry and exit points.

8. Sketch and photograph the incident site (the squad leader controls and makes an intermediate and pinpoint sketch of the incident site; the tracker and team leader sketch, photograph, and document any evidence made by the quarry).

9. Interview witnesses or tactically question hostiles.
10. Radio an initial tracker nine-line to the TCE.
11. Conduct a quick briefing to the squad to ensure that everyone knows the information contained within the tracker situation report; any units and assets supporting the tracking operation; and any primary, alternate, contingency, and emergency (PACE) plans.
12. Begin the operation.

Important information needed before conducting the tracking operation covers who, what, where, when, why, and how.

- **Who** and how many individuals are to be followed? Are they enemy or friendly?
- **What** occurred at the incident site? Was it an ambush? Was it a mortar or rocket attack? What were the types of footwear impressions made by the quarry recovered from the incident site? Are there indicators of what weapon systems the enemy is carrying?
- **Where** did the incident occur? What are the grid coordinates to the incident site? From what direction did the quarry come and in what direction did it go?
- **When** did the incident occur? What time did the incident happen? How much lead time does the enemy have on the tracker conducting the pursuit?
- **Why** did the incident happen?
- **How** did the incident happen?

The answers to these questions provide the tracker squad with the necessary information to relay to the TCE in the nine-line. Once the situation report has been passed on and acknowledged, the team is ready to conduct the operation.

THE OPERATION
Tracking operations are best conducted using multiple squads. The objective of the operation is to close the time-distance gap between

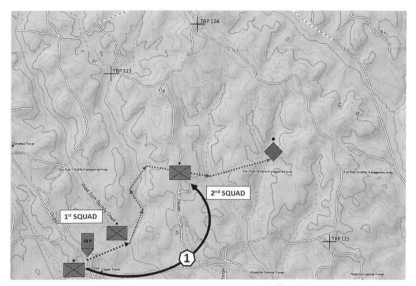

The first combat tracking squad initiates the pursuit while the second squad bounds forward along the enemy's direction of travel and cuts for sign. If the second squad finds the enemy's tracks, then it becomes the lead squad.

the pursuit force and the quarry. The only way to do this quickly, effectively, and efficiently is to employ two or more squads to the task. The squads use bounding tactics to close with or cut off the enemy's escape.

At the initial start point, the first squad that will lead the operation conducts any necessary coordinations with the on-ground commander and exploits the incident site to determine the who, what, where, when, why, and how. After completing this, and when it is able to determine the size of the quarry, the footprint impressions they will be following, and the direction taken by the quarry, the squad contacts the TCE to report an initial tracker nine-line.

The lead tracker squad initiates the pursuit, with the support group following at a distance that won't give away the trackers' position but is close enough to provide support should the squad make enemy contact. Whenever the quarry's direction changes, the

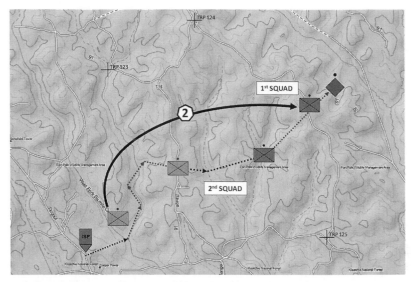

The first combat tracking squad breaks off pursuit and bounds past the second squad.

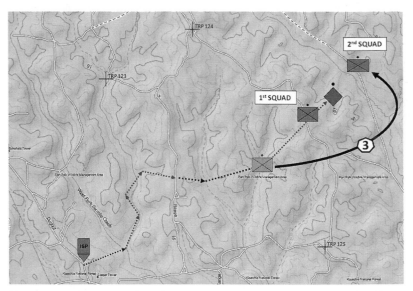

The process is repeated to close the time-distance gap. If the bounding squad does not detect sign along the enemy's line of travel, the enemy is likely boxed in.

squad leader radios a new tracker nine-line, reporting only the changes. Once the quarry has developed a pattern and a good direction of travel has been assessed, the second combat tracker squad leaps forward to a location that may present a track trap (such as a trail or road that crosses the enemy's direction of travel) to search for sign. If the bounding squad detects and confirms the enemy's tracks and ascertains that the enemy group is still intact and has not split up, it reports that it has done so and then becomes the lead tracking squad.

The squad that initiated the operation may then be told to break off their track line and move to a pick-up site to bound forward to another location to cut for enemy sign. The cycle repeats: The lead tracking squad determines a pattern in the enemy's direction of travel and the bounding squad moves to a new location to search for sign.

If after several cycles no sign has been detected, that means the enemy is most likely boxed in. In this case, the squad following the track line must be prepared to radio the support group immediately should the enemy be sighted or contact occur.

5

Countertracking, Mines, and Booby Traps

"There is nothing that sharpens a man's senses so acutely as to know that bitter and determined enemies are in pursuit of him night and day."
—Fredrick Russell Burnham,
from Scouting on Two Continents

Combat tracker units conducting a pursuit must realize that if the quarry is aware he is being hunted, he will likely employ some kind of maneuver to counter the tracker. Countertracking techniques are used primarily to slow down, confuse, lose, or eliminate a tracker. Culture, religious affiliation, and the amount and quality of training the quarry received will determine how he reacts to the pressure of being hunted. It's important that the tracker identify when the quarry is attempting to use countertracking techniques and record and report the methods. Sharing this information with other teams will prevent them from being deceived and could save lives.

The enemy who is conducting countertracking will never attempt to:

- Walk on anything he can step over
- Cut what he can break naturally
- Break what he can bend
- Bend what he can move
- Move anything when he can get through without moving it
- Step on soft ground when he can walk on something hard

• Create a definitive pattern of his intentions
• Do anything needlessly

Countertracking techniques can be broken down into three basic categories: speed and distance, deception, and offensive.

SPEED AND DISTANCE

The speed and distance technique is when the quarry tries to move at a quicker pace than his pursuers. Although this technique may be effective for short distances, it usually creates problems for the quarry. By moving more quickly, the quarry will create more sign, making the track line easier to follow. He will also make more noise, tire faster, and become psychologically stressed from being pursued; as a result, his total situational awareness will become degraded. If the quarry is a group, these problems will be worse, especially if one of the members is wounded or not able to keep up with the others. The quarry's use of this technique will ultimately be a tactical advantage for tracker units, assuming they can keep up momentum and pressure.

DECEPTION

The combat tracker needs to have a full understanding of the types of deception an enemy might employ and be able to identify indicators of this deception without losing ground during a pursuit. The tracker should remember that the quarry might use one or a combination of deception methods.

Walking Backwards. This is normally employed where the ground is soft and footprints can be easily identified. When the quarry walks backwards, he is attempting to conceal his true direction of movement. Indicators of this method show a shortened stride. As well, the contact phase of a backward step will begin with the toe and ball of the foot, which will appear more pronounced than the heel. Also, loose dirt and debris will be dragged forward in

Walking backwards

the direction of travel; ground vegetation will be trampled or bent down pointing in the direction of movement.

Camouflaging Sign. The enemy may attempt to disguise his impressions by wrapping footwear with cloth or using soft-soled footwear that leaves less distinctive impressions that may appear older. The quarry may also switch footwear so that the impressions have different tread patterns that could confuse pursuers. The enemy may also fabricate footwear that leaves impressions resembling wild animal sign (trackers shouldn't be fooled by this method since most large animals have four legs).

The enemy may use small sections of carpet to cross a trail or road, laying down one piece and stepping on it, then laying down another and stepping on it and so on. To detect this, a tracker should notice the outline impressions of the carpet or the marks left by picking them up. The enemy may sprinkle birdseed over tracks crossing a road in an attempt to attract wildlife that will contaminate the track line (the remnants of the birdseed will always remain, however).

The enemy may attempt to camouflage his sign and confuse or lose a tracker by entering a populated area or traveling along frequently used trails, paths, or roads. This method works best when the quarry knows the daily patterns of the local population and uses them to conceal his movements; for example, he might travel in front of a cattle or goat herder who moves along a path at a certain time every day. To detect this deception, the tracker must be persistent and identify the "jump-off" point, where he can then resume the pursuit.

Brushing out tracks still leaves activity indicators.

Brushing Out Tracks. The enemy will use this method when trying to conceal his movements in areas that capture good impressions. The tracker will often see this method used when the quarry has crossed a trail or road or moved up or down an embankment. When the quarry attempts to brush out his tracks, the sign the tracker was following will disappear—but the area that has been brushed out will stand out from its surroundings. It can be identified by either the disturbance or its distinct color change.

Walking Along a Log. The quarry may attempt to walk across a log or large piece of deadfall lying across or alongside the direction of travel so as not to leave any sign of the direction change. To detect this, the tracker should be able to locate bruised vegetation and damaged, scuffed, or broken bark as well as any material transferred to the log. He should also be able to identify where the quarry jumped off the log.

Moving Along a Fence Line. Some pursued groups have used fence lines to travel a hundred meters or more—but this should not fool the tracker. If the sign being followed suddenly disappears and there is a fence nearby, look at it carefully. The wire may appear stretched or rust may have been rubbed off where handholds were used. And at some point along the fence the tracker should find where the quarry jumped off.

Stone Hopping. The method of moving from stone to stone is an attempt to leave no impressions in the dirt's surface. It may also be used when crossing a stream or river. To detect this deception, the tracker should be able to identify disturbances around the stone. A stone that has remained in the same position for a long period of time will have dirt and sand built up around its base because of the effects of weather. When the stone is stepped on, the material around the base will crack or crumble and a "shadow" will appear around the stone's base. Scuffs or scratches may be made or debris transferred to the stone surface.

Walking Over Hard Ground. The quarry may attempt to move over hard surfaces to reduce the amount of sign left behind. A careful assessment of the area will help a tracker determine where the quarry went; the tracker should check potential track traps on the edge of the area of hard ground to attempt to locate the quarry's exit from the hard surface.

Walking Through a Stream. To escape pursuit, the quarry may attempt to cross rivers and streams or move through a stream with a fast-flowing current or where the river may be murky. Depending on the terrain, as well as the amount of time since the quarry passed through, this can sometimes allow the quarry to leave little or no immediately visible sign.

In water where the current is almost nonexistent and the water clear, tracking is possible. Look for water color change due to disturbances within the riverbed or aerial disturbances at the exit point made when the quarry moved through reeds, long grass, or brush.

In streams where there is a fast current, the sign will undoubtedly have been washed away. The tracker will have to extend his search in order to locate the quarry's exit point.

Dropping Off. The drop-off technique is used when the quarry is a group and attempts to lessen its sign signature over a period of time and distance by having one individual at a time split off from the group at irregular intervals. Individuals will continue to split away from the group along the direction of travel until little sign is evident. (The quarry may then move to a designated rally point to regroup.) The tracker shouldn't be fooled by this technique—he should notice that the amount of sign he is following is decreasing. Flankers should notice sign from the departing quarry that will likely cross their paths.

Bombshelling. This method involves the quarry group splitting into two or more smaller groups. When bombshelling is identified, the tracker should follow the sign that is the most prominent while reporting the location of the separation point to allow the commander to deploy another tracker unit.

Remember that when a drop-off or bombshelling technique is identified, the team needs to ask themselves *why* this has occurred. If the quarry is an organized military unit, they may know they are being hunted and are becoming desperate; they may have split temporarily to regroup at a different location. If the enemy is an insurgent force, there may be other explanations of why they split: because they know they are being hunted or because they are returning to their homes or villages. Or there might have been two or more insurgent groups coming together to accomplish a task and then returning to areas of control or safety.

Doubling Back. This is when the quarry attempts to throw the tracker off by laying a track line in the general direction of travel before walking backwards along the same line to a jump-off point. This technique is often combined with other methods to conceal the jump-off point: brushing out tracks, stone hopping, or walking

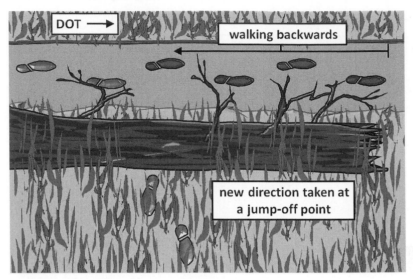

Walking backwards to a jump-off point.

along a log. The quarry's intent is to cause the tracker to continue along the false trail until he loses the sign without realizing the quarry jumped off.

TYPICAL DECEPTION SCENARIOS

The following scenarios illustrate a few common attempts to shake off pursuers. Efficient trackers must be aware of the different ways a quarry will try to escape contact.

Change of Direction at a Big Tree. When moving from a thickly vegetated area to a more open area, the quarry walks past a big tree toward a semi-open area for up to ten paces before attepting to walk backwards to the forward side of the tree. He then makes a 90-degree change in direction, passing the tree on the forward side. He then may change direction again 50 to 100 meters farther. The goal is to draw the tracker away from the tree and down the wrong path.

Cut-the-Corner Deception. The quarry uses this technique when approaching a known road or trail intersection. About 100 meters from the road, he changes direction 45 degrees to the left or

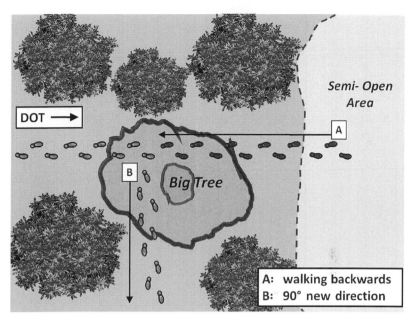

Change of direction at a big tree

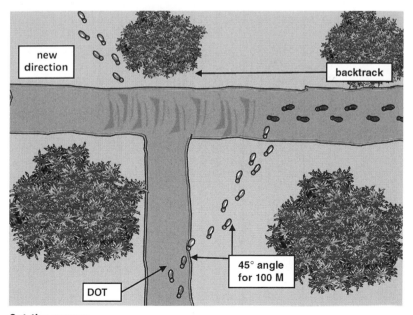

Cut-the-corner

right. When he reaches the road, he purposely leaves obvious sign down the road in the direction of the deception and then attempts to walk backwards along the track line to the point where he entered the road. He then moves in the opposite direction of the false trail, attempting to leave as little sign as possible. Once the quarry has moved the desired distance and located a suitable jump-off point, he changes direction and continues forward.

Slip-the-Stream Deception. The quarry uses this technique when approaching a known stream. It's similar to the cut-the-corner technique. The quarry makes a 45-degree change of direction just before reaching the stream. He enters the water and moves upstream so that floating debris will head downstream and cover the direction and exit point. (The quarry may create a false exit point with a false trail leading away from the stream—to do so, he must walk backward to the exit point and reenter the stream.)

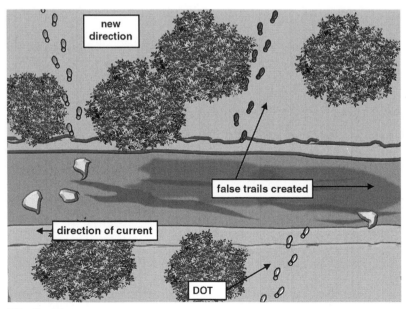

Slip-the-stream

The quarry then moves downstream to another exit point before changing direction. Tributaries offer the quarry other alternatives to confuse the tracker.

The quarry may also use any combination of the following maneuvers: keeping in the center of the stream in deep water, exiting the water where banks are not covered with moss or vegetation, walking out backwards onto soft ground, walking up vegetation-covered tributaries and then attempting to replace the vegetation in its natural position, or traveling downstream until coming to the main river and escaping by floating downriver on a log or prepositioned boat.

The slip-the-stream scenario will often slow down the tracker temporarily, but, with common sense, he can reacquire the right track, especially if he keeps in mind that soil along stream and river banks is usually soft and will crumble or capture slide or skid marks when someone leaves or enters the water. It's helpful to remember that a quarry exiting a stream will leave behind two types of sign: 1) water draining from pants and boots and 2) mud from the stream transferred onto stones and grass. Also look for overhanging moss-covered branches, which will usually be wet; if the quarry uses them as handholds when exiting the water the bark will crumble or scuff easily.

Step Technique. The step technique is nothing more than the quarry attempting to change his route by making a series of 90-degree turns about every 100 to 200 meters.

Skip Method. In this method, while moving single file, a quarry group stops and attempts to move carefully 20 to 30 meters to the left or right flank. The quarry also tries to camoflage the jump-off point by returning disturbed vegetation to its original position. Sometimes, one or two members of the group create a false trail to confuse the tracking unit.

Angle Technique. The quarry makes a series of random angled direction changes in an attempt to shake off pursuers.

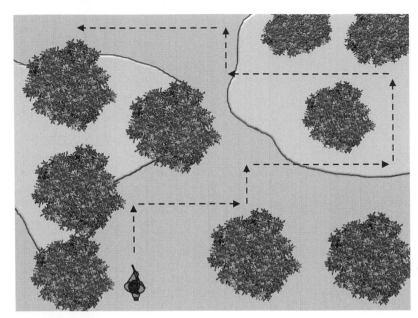

Step technique

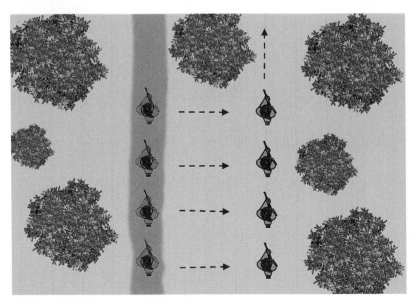

Skip method

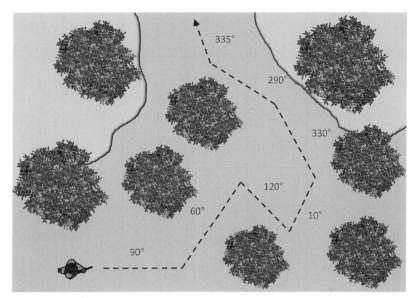

Angle technique

OFFENSIVE TECHNIQUES

Offensive techniques involve the use of ambushes or booby traps designed to eliminate, slow down, or discourage a tracker squad.

The Fishhook. In this technique, the quarry doubles back on his own track line to an overwatch position, where he can observe the back trail and ambush pursuing trackers. If the quarry is a large group, some may ambush the pursuers to cover the escape of the main group.

The Circle. This technique is often used by an enemy attempting to hide in a snow-covered environment, but it can be modified and used in any terrain. The enemy lays a false trail in a large circle that starts from a road or trail and returns to the same point. At some point along the track line, the quarry will attempt to step off the trail, leaving one set of tracks. The quarry may use other countertracking techniques, such as the "big tree," to conceal the track line that splits off from the circle. And one member of the quarry group may attempt to brush out or camouflage the tracks. The

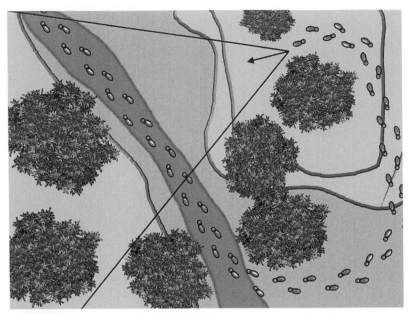

The fishhook

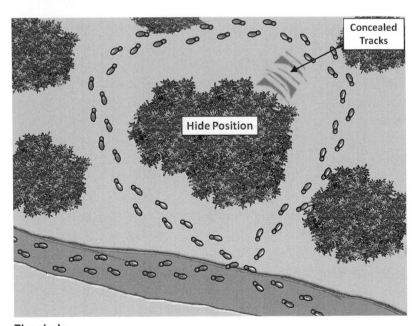

The circle

quarry may use this technique to fool his pursuers into bypassing him, or to lay an ambush for the pursuers.

The Box or Figure-Eight. The quarry sets out on a set course for a certain distance, then makes a 90-degree turn to change

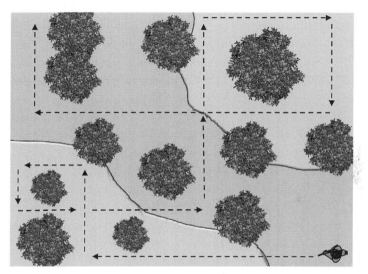

The box

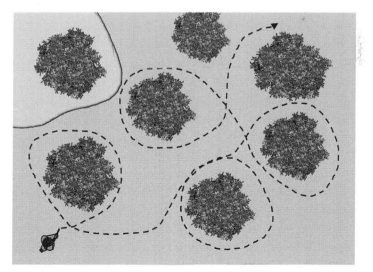

The figure-eight

direction. He will continue the same distance, then make another 90-degree turn, and so on to make a box. He may try to discourage pursuers by employing some type of booby trap along his back trail or attempt to ambush the tracking unit. In a similar maneuver, the quarry moves in a figure-eight pattern instead of a box.

MINES AND BOOBY TRAPS

Mines and booby traps are typically employed by conventional forces as a means of defense. History has shown, however, that irregular forces will employ mines and booby traps in an offensive manner—to harass and lower the morale of opposing forces

by inflicting casualties and destroying or damaging equipment.

Mines are usually triggered by their victims and intended to damage their targets by the blast itself and/or the resulting fragments. A booby trap is an explosive or nonexplosive trap designed to kill or injure its victim, incapacitate or destroy equipment, or provide an early warning to the enemy. These improvised devices can be either technically simple or extremely sophisticated. They are popular in insurgencies because they're easy to construct and can be used almost anywhere at little or no cost.

Almost anything can be booby-trapped—buildings, weapons, dead bodies, and common everyday items—and many techniques can be used to detonate them: trip wires, electronic initiation, traction, tension, pressure, and magnetic or seismic fuses. Booby traps are usually camouflaged and weatherized to prevent detection and unintentional detonation. Some booby traps, especially mines, may be employed with anti-handling devices attached.

Typically, booby traps fall into one of two categories. *Nonexplosive booby traps* include spike traps, ditches, and craters. Holes are dug—with the depth and size being dependent on the intended target—and filled with sharpened sticks, barbs, nails, coils, or other sharp items intended to inflict injury or damage. *Explosive booby traps* (or improvised explosive devices) are the most common booby traps, made in a wide variety of shapes and sizes, depending on their intended purpose.

HOW THEY ARE EMPLOYED
Likely locations for mines that use a pressure firing system include road junctions, bypasses, wheel tracks, approaches to bridges, rough or newly repaired roads, culverts, narrow roads between restrictive terrain, and along the sides of roads flanked by fields. Antipersonnel mines are typically employed above ground or slightly underground. An enemy who is being aggressively pursued can be expected to use antipersonnel mines to discourage pursuit. If trip wires are used, they are usually stretched 3 to 5 inches above ground and composed of a monofilament "fishing line" type of wire.

The explosive charges used in booby traps are generally the same as those used in mines. Standard antitank and antipersonnel mines, grenades, mortar and artillery projectiles, and miscellaneous improvised explosive charges are all used in booby traps.

The tracker must be aware that *any* area the quarry may have occupied is potentially mined and/or booby-trapped. Buildings, especially those used as safe houses, offer almost limitless places for explosive booby traps: entrances, furniture, windows, floorboards, and all sorts of miscellaneous items.

Areas in and around villages may also be booby-trapped by the quarry before they withdraw: gates, fences and hedges, trails and paths, shrines, wells, dead bodies, abandoned supplies, and equipment such as weapons, ammunition, clothing, and food. *All discarded equipment—as well as caches—must be approached with caution.*

Nonexplosive booby traps have the same purpose as explosive booby traps—to inflict casualties and hinder the progress of the operation. Nearly all nonexplosive devices are improvised from locally available materials and take advantage of natural camouflage. They may be employed along with mines or explosive booby traps. A tracker must not be so focused on looking for trip wires that he overlooks a well-camouflaged nonexplosive trap—the enemy knows that these traps are most effective when the pursuers are in a hurry and careless.

VISUAL INDICATORS
A variety of indicators could alert the tracker to the presence of mines or booby traps. These include:

- Trip wires
- Electrical wires
- Aiming markers of natural or manmade materials
- Loose dirt
- Sinkholes in regular shapes

- Exposed metal objects protruding from the ground
- Signs of road repair, such as holes filled with other material
- Out-of-place or wilted vegetation
- Objects that appear out of place
- Changes in local patterns of life
- Items that attract attention, such as military equipment as souvenirs

The enemy will likely indicate the placement of mines and booby traps somehow, even if the indicator is not obvious to the untrained eye. If he didn't mark them, the movement of locals and people friendly to him would be unacceptably curtailed, and roads and trails would be effectively blocked.

When the enemy is overpowered quickly, many of these indicators are likely to still be in place. Although such indicators can vary widely, some examples will help the observant tracker spot possible mines and booby trap locations. Indicators of possible mines or booby traps include:

- Sticks placed on a road or trail arranged like an arrow to indicate the presence of mines or booby traps, or to indicate the far limit of the danger area (the direction of the arrow does not always indicate the direction of the mine, however, and an arrangement of markers may sometimes be used down the trail from the arrow)
- Stake marker: a wooden branch 6 to 8 inches long placed into the ground at about a 45-degree angle with the end of the stick pointing toward the mine or booby trap

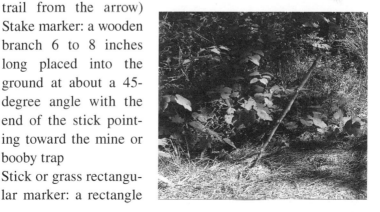

- Stick or grass rectangular marker: a rectangle

consisting of four sticks forming a box around the device. A variation is bunches of tied grass at each corner of the square to mark the device.

- Tripod marker consisting of three stick legs lashed together to form a tripod, which is then placed over the device to indicate its location
- Broken brush: the top of a small sapling will be broken and stripped of most of the leaves and branches from the tip; it's then pointed down toward the device
- A stick broken at a right angle and laid across the road or trail.
- A leaf folded lengthwise in half with a thin stick approximately the thickness of a toothpick woven through the leaves in two places
- A forked stick driven into the ground with another stick laid into the fork may point toward the danger (this arrangement might also indicate direction of movement)
- Large leaf and stick combination markers: two large leaves are sometimes placed parallel to each other on top of the device, or two short stakes are placed on the trail in front and to the rear of the device (these markers may be used individually or together)
- Parallel stick marker: short sticks are laid parallel to the road or trail to indicate that the trail is free of devices
- Rock markers: various formations (circles, pyramids, straight lines) of rocks placed along roads or trails
- Spaced stick or stone marker: three stakes or stones, one on each side of the road and one in the middle
- Vehicle track markers: because their adversaries often follow old vehicle tracks, the enemy will place devices within the tracks or ruts, which are sometimes marked with crossed sticks or an arrangement of small rocks. The location of the device in relation to the markers is not consistent—it could be under the marker or further on.

- X marker: stakes placed in four corners or sticks forming an X
- Vine markers: loops of vines or vegetation are sometimes placed about 6 inches from a mine in a grassy area alongside a trail. This marker will blend with the existing vegetation and can be difficult to detect
- A cloverleaf shape made from natural material, with the stems pointing in the same direction
- A series of palm leaves bent to form a uniform pattern
- Instantaneous grenade fuse markings: grenades without delay elements may be marked with a dot of paint on the grenade body (the dots may not have a specific color pattern so long as the device can be identified by the person who marked it)
- Short pieces of string placed at or above entrances to dwellings, caves, and tunnels may indicate booby traps, and the string will likely be inconspicuous to the casual observer
- Goalpost marker: two sticks stuck vertically into the ground with a third stick lashed horizontally to the other two, forming a goalpost (the structure may be anywhere from 6 to 18 inches high)

DETECTION

Detecting mines and booby traps requires constant alertness and careful observation. The efficiency of detection efforts depends on the knowledge of the devices commonly used by the enemy. All trackers should be trained to detect mines or booby traps in the normal conduct of their duties. Methods and techniques for doing so are given here.

- Do not wear sunglasses: Sunglasses have been shown to reduce the ability to detect trip wires and camouflaged devices.
- Be alert for trip wires across trails, along shoulders of roads, in likely ambush sites, across the most accessible route through dense vegetation, at the approaches to and within villages, in

and around likely helicopter landing sites, at the approaches to insurgent positions, across dikes, and at bridges, fords, and ditches.

- Look for mud smears, grass, sticks, dirt, animal dung, or other substances on roads—all are indicators of possible mines or booby traps.
- Look for evidence of apparent road repair, such as new filling or paving, road patches, and culvert work. Such areas often conceal explosive devices.
- If possible, avoid tire marks, ruts, or skid marks along roads; these areas may conceal explosive devices.
- Be alert for any signs placed in or on trees, posts, and stakes, or painted on roadways. Most of these signs are inconspicuous, and although not all of them indicate the presence of an explosive device, they should be considered as a possible marking device.
- Watch for wires leading away from the side of the road. Although the enemy will usually bury command firing wires, some may be only partially buried or not at all.
- Be alert for suspicious items in trees, branches, or bushes, including hand grenades or mortar or artillery rounds. Trip wires across the trail may be difficult to detect, but the device itself might be more noticeable.
- Watch for any feature of the terrain that does not appear natural, such as uprooted and cut vegetation that has dried and changed color, for example. Also remember that rain may wash away some of the material used to cover a device, partially exposing it, or material covering pits can sink, leaving a depression or a crack around the edges, indicating an excavation. Tops placed over pits and traps may appear as unusual mounds with uniform dimensions.
- Observe the locals, particularly in areas that have been occupied by the enemy. They usually know the locations of the devices placed in and around their villages and will avoid

those areas by walking along only one side of the road or in the middle of a road, avoiding the sides and shoulders. They may also avoid a particular road entirely. As well, locals may avoid using certain buildings or facilities within their village— a good indicator that those buildings may be mined or booby trapped.

- Remember that enemy supplies and equipment are frequently booby trapped, especially caches that have been left behind.
- Be aware of potential souvenir items that may be booby trapped, such as firearms, bags or backpacks, and uniforms and miscellaneous items of clothing and equipment.
- Nonexplosive traps placed at or above ground level are usually well camouflaged but can be detected by careful observation. Spike-board plates (used to deflate tires) may be partially concealed in the grass but the vegetation will appear straight and uniform compared to the irregular pattern of the grass surrounding it. If nails or wires are used as spikes, they may shine in the sun. The "log and ball mace" and suspended spikes are of such size and configuration that they will appear unnatural among the trees branches—with careful observation overhead you can detect these devices.
- Pieces of wood (boards or bamboo) or other debris on the road may indicate the presence of pressure-firing devices for anti-tank or antipersonnel mines. These may be either placed on the road's surface or partially buried and camouflaged. Hasty emplacement of the device or weather conditions often reduces the effectiveness of the camouflage, allowing the device to be detected by careful observation. Vehicle operators should never drive over wood, sticks, or other debris on the road.

COUNTER-MINE, -BOOBY TRAP, AND -IED PRINCIPLES
- Maintain an offensive mindset at all times
- Develop and maintain situational awareness
- Stay observant

- Avoid setting patterns
- Maintain 360 degrees of security
- Maintain standoff when a possible device has been encountered
- Maintain tactical dispersion
- Use protective cover from potential blast and fragmentation
- Use technology to mitigate the threat when possible

REPORTING

The nine-line IED/unexploded ordnance (UXO) report is radioed to the TCE whenever a relevant device has been detected and needs to be reported. The nine-line serves to alert other units to the threat as well as allow personnel who are trained to exploit and dismantle the devices to be sent.

Line 1. DATE-TIME GROUP (DTG):	When was the item discovered?
Line 2. REPORT ACTIVITY AND LOCATION:	Unit and grid location of the IED/UXO.
Line 3. CONTACT METHOD:	Radio frequency, call signs, point of contact, and telephone number.
Line 4. TYPE OF ORDNANCE:	Dropped, projected, placed, or thrown; the number of items if there are more than one.
Line 5. NUCLEAR, BIOLOGICAL, CHEMICAL CONTAMINATION:	Be as specific as possible.
Line 6. RESOURCES THREATENED:	Equipment, facilities, or other assets that are threatened.
Line 7. IMPACT ON MISSION:	Short description of current tactical situation and how the device affects the status of the mission.
Line 8. PROTECTIVE MEASURES:	Any protective measures taken to protect personnel and equipment.
Line 9. RECOMMENDED PRIORITY:	Immediate, indirect, minor, or no threat.

"THE FIVE CS"

The five Cs are conducted in no specific order, but the response must be instinctive, effective, and based on METT-T factors (mission, enemy, troops available, terrain, and time):

Confirm. The presence of the suspected device should be confirmed. This needs to be done from a safe location with protective cover. Binoculars and scopes are used to confirm from a distance—*always maintain a safe distance from the suspected device.* Be aware and observant for the possibility of secondary devices. Do not get tunnel vision. Inform the rest of the unit of the presence of the suspected item.

Clear. All personnel are to be moved away from the suspect item. The patrol leader at the scene makes the decision as to how large an area is to be cleared. Personnel should make maximum use of hard protective cover, ensuring they are out of the direct line of sight from the suspect area. If cover cannot be obtained, distance from the device should be maximized.

Cordon. The area of the device is to be cordoned off and an incident control point established. The purpose of the cordon is to prevent unauthorized personnel from entering the site, and to preserve the scene for further exploitation as well as to provide outward protection and security against command-initiated IEDs.

Check. All personnel should check the immediate area for possible devices by conducting 5- and 25-meter sweeps from their positions. Individuals should look for the indicators of a device—detonation cord, receiver, transmitter, cell phone, antenna, and so on—that may lead to other IEDs flanking the unit. Any suspicious items should be reported to the patrol leader immediately.

Control. The area inside the cordon is controlled to ensure only authorized access. Allow only first responders to breach the cordon through the ICP. All other traffic should be diverted away from the cordon.

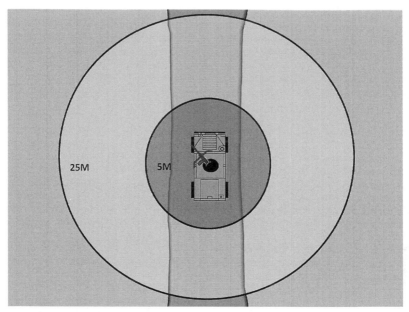

5- and 25-meter drillls

CONDUCTING 5- AND 25-METER DRILLS

The 5- and 25-meter drills ensure the patrol stops in a safe place. They require the entire vehicle crew to read the terrain and avoid areas likely to conceal IEDs, mines, and/or UXOs.

The initial check is conducted from within the protection of the vehicle. Identify the best position to stop then carry out a standoff check using binoculars or other optics. Check for disturbed earth and suspicious objects. Work from ground level up to above head height. Once the vehicle is stopped, conduct an immediate physical check of the ground before dismounting. Then check around and under the vehicle. Then clear the area out to 5 meters around the vehicle. Be systematic and take your time.

Once 5-meter checks are completed, continue scanning out to 25 meters in your sector or area of responsibility, checking for potential IED indicators and anything else out of the ordinary. If searching off the road, scan the area first with optics for possible devices. Be on the lookout for potential triggermen observing your actions.

Remain calm upon identifying an IED—hasty actions may alert the triggerman. While stationary, remain observant out beyond the 25-meter distance and observe for potential threats. Retain situational awareness.

When reacting to a situation where a device was initiated and personnel are wounded, always advance cautiously when attempting to render aid. Do not rush to any wounded individuals. There could be a secondary device in the vicinity. The man nearest each casualty should carefully clear his way to the individual and render first aid. Under no circumstances should leaders or others crowd near or around the wounded individuals. Conduct a brief but careful search for other explosive devices in the immediate vicinity before moving on.

ROUTE CLEARING
The combat tracker squad may have to clear suspicious areas along hostile borders, trails, or roads for potential mines, booby traps, or

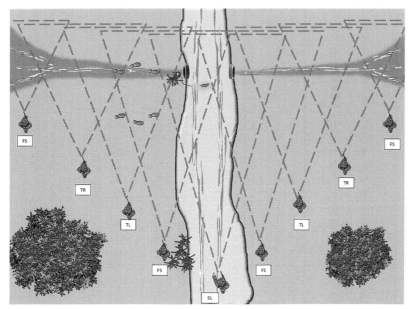

Clearing a route

ambushes. The squad deploys and clears along the suspected route, observing for enemy indicators, using optics that will provide the squad standoff should it detect a device. The squad conducts its search by deploying into a V formation with 20 to 30 meters between squad members along both sides of the road. The squad scans with optics, looking for suspected enemy activity indicators or possible ambush locations. It patrols forward cautiously. The object is to detect either the enemy or a device using optics from a safe distance.

The team should implement an internal signal to alert other members that a device has been detected without alerting the enemy. If a device is detected, the squad cautiously backtracks out of the area to a safe distance, and the squad leader notifies the on-ground commander or reports a UXO/IED nine-line to his higher-up.

TRACKING WITH
LIMITED VISIBILITY

Technological advances have made it possible to track at night using artificial light sources and night-vision devices. With these, the tracker is able to manipulate the light source to produce the best angle to view tracks. Each type of artificial light source has

advantages and dis-advantages, however, and so some are more useful to the tracker than others.

If the tracker uses a flashlight, the light shouldn't be so bright that it ruins his night vision. The flashlight needs be durable and create a beam of light that isn't too intense. It also needs to have a long battery life. Flashlights used in law enforcement and close-quarters battle work are not very practical since the beam of light they produce is too bright and the batteries tend to drain quickly. The best type of flashlight is a durable AA or AAA light with different colored filter lenses (AA and AAA batteries are relatively easy to find anywhere in the world).

Many flashlights use standard incandescent bulbs. These are cheap to make and are the dimmest of all bulbs. Xenon incandescent bulbs offer better brightness over other incandescents.

From left to right: Incandescent, xenon, and LED bulbs.

LED bulbs are brighter than incandescent bulbs and have a longer lifespan and use less energy. LEDs are available in a variety of colors: white, red, green, and cyan (blue). LED flashlights will typically contain one bulb for focused light or an array of bulbs for increased brightness.

Infrared light sources can be used to augment the available ambient light for conversion by night-vision devices, increasing visibility without using a visible light source. (Note that the use of infrared light with night-vision devices should not be confused with thermal imaging. The difference is that thermal imagers create images by detecting heat, or infrared radiation, that radiates

from the surface of an object and its surroundings.)

ChemLights, produced by Cyalume Technologies, come in many different sizes and colors (including infrared) and are part of the military supply system.

COLORED LENSES

The military has traditionally used red light for working at night, but with the increased use of night-vision devices, it is now using more green light for military applications. Green light offers some advantages over red: The human eye is more receptive to green light, and we achieve better visual acuity than when using red light.

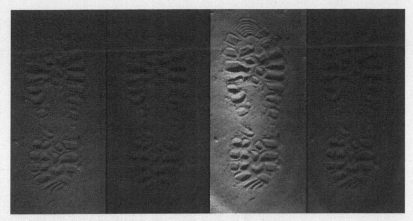

From left to right: White, red, green, and blue light.

Green also allows a tracker to differentiate between other colors that red does not—useful when reading a map at night, for instance.

NIGHT-VISION DEVICES

Two types of night-vision devices can enhance the tracker's capability at night: image enhancers and thermal imagers. Image enhancers operate by collecting a tiny amount of light and amplifying it until objects are easily seen. They are the most common type of night-vision device and rely on an image-intensifier tube to collect and amplify infrared and visible light.

Generation 0 image enhancers use an active infrared beam projected by the device to detect objects. They are known to distort images, however, and have a short image-intensifier tube life. Generation I enhancers use ambient light provided by the moon and stars to enhance the normal amount of reflected infrared light within the environment. They use the same image-intensifier tube technology as do generation 0s, so image distortion and short image-intensifier tube life are still concerns.

Generation II enhancers feature improved resolution and performance over generation I devices, and are more reliable. The biggest improvement is the ability to see in extremely low-light conditions; images viewed with these devices are significantly less distorted and brighter than with earlier-generation models. Generation III enhancers offer better resolution and sensitivity, and generation IV enhancers feature significant improvements that allow them to react to fluctuations in lighting conditions quickly. This capability is a critical advance because it allows the user to quickly move from high-light to low-light or from low-light to high-light environments without adverse effects.

Thermal imagers operate by detecting the heat radiating from objects. Hotter objects will emit more of this light than cooler objects. Thermal imagers are capable of revealing areas that have been disturbed by humans. The law enforcement community has used these devices with great success over the years to discover discarded or cached items left by criminals.

DISADVANTAGES

The main problem trackers working at night face is retaining their natural night vision based on the actual amount of illumination they use and not the color of the light itself. The more intense the light, the more it will negatively affect night vision—both the ability to see and the amount of time it takes to regain natural night vision—regardless of whether the light used is white, red, green, or blue. Although trackers might have the ability to track at night, depending on the tactical situation, it could be either beneficial or detrimental to the mission to do so. In some cases, it wisest to mark the last sign and move off the track line to conduct patrol-base activities for the night. Understanding the enemy and the tracking environment will help the squad determine whether or not the benefits of tracking at night outweigh the risks to the squad's security.

Depending on the tracking environment as well as the tracker's training in the use of night vision and infrared light sources, tracking at night could slow down the pursuit, particularly if the track line is lost or contaminated. As well, the tracker and rest of the squad may violate their own security by creating noise when pursuing their quarry through difficult terrain at night, thus increasing the odds of being ambushed.

The use of a flashlight will speed up the process, but the unit could possibly give away its position by doing so. The question the unit needs to ask is: Who walks around in the middle of the night with a white, red, green, or blue flashlight? If the only answer is "military personnel," then this may not be a good option. But if it is common for locals to move at night with dull white flashlights, then it may be acceptable to continue the pursuit so long as the tracker uses the same type of light source used by the locals.

URBAN TRACKING

Conducting tracking operations in urban areas poses unique challenges, but, in general, the times a tracker will need to perform his duties in an urban area are going to be limited to those instances when he has followed a track line from a rural area to a village, small outpost, or similarly populated area. And tracking techniques used in rural environments can also be used in urban environments. Still, infrastructure differences—such as concrete and asphalt roads as opposed to dirt trails—provide an entirely new medium upon which sign must be identified.

During a tracking operation in a built-up environment, security will be critical. The tracker support group will provide that security, allowing the entire combat tracker squad to search for and follow the enemy's sign.

Urban areas are classified into four categories: *villages* (with populations of three thousand or fewer), *strip areas* (urban areas built along roads connecting towns or cities), *towns or small cities* (with populations of up to one hundred thousand and not part of a major urban complex), and *large cities* with associated urban sprawls (population can be in the millions, covering hundreds of square kilometers).

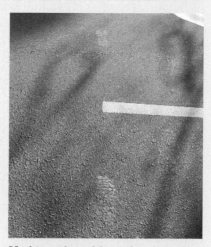

INDICATORS AND TRACK TRAPS

When searching for indicators and locating enemy sign in urban areas, the ability to find and use track traps is critical. Examples of track traps within urban areas include:

Mud transferred from the quarry's shoes onto pavement.

- Edges of roads
- Roadside curbs where dust and dirt collect
- Along alleyways
- Banks of streams, rivers, and culverts
- In and around gardens
- Areas that have gathered early-morning dew
- Along inclines and declines
- Oil spots in parking areas
- Soft tar
- Construction and other work sites
- Drainage ditches

Edges of roads collect dust, dirt, and debris, making them good track traps.

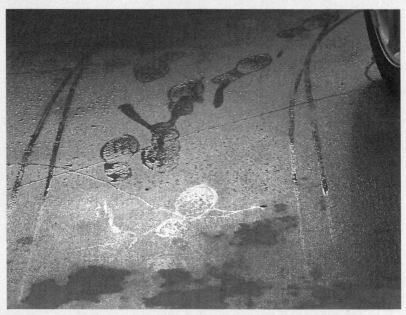

The quarry's footprints are captured in morning dew on concrete.

A track trap along an incline and walkway

Oil from a parking lot transferred to a parking block by the quarry's shoes

- Muddy areas
- Sports fields and children's play areas
- Dump sites
- Vacant lots
- Bicycle routes or trails
- Exercise routes
- Repaired roadways or other surfaces
- Entrances to doorways and gates
- Along fence lines and walls
- Edges of irrigated areas

A track trap along a walking path. Track traps are often farther apart in urban environments than in rural ones.

In an urban environment, the same principles of tracking apply as in a rural environment. What changes is that the combat tracker squad will have to be more creative and demonstrate more initiative because of the complexity of the environment. The squad will most likely have to cover longer distances over paved or concrete surfaces and search a multitude of possible directions to find out which way the enemy traveled. Older villages and towns with poorly maintained infrastructures will provide more opportunities for locating track traps than more modern and developed cities.

Once a direction of travel has been determined, the tracker team breaks down into smaller elements and moves forward along roads and intersecting alleyways, searching for track traps along the avenues likely used by the enemy. When the squad is faced with one or more options as to the enemy's direction, a minimum two men (one tracker and one cover man) search one of the possible directions. When the sign is reacquired, the rest of the team is notified, and the search process resumes. Using a leap-frog technique, moving from track trap to track trap, the squad is able to cover ground more quickly.

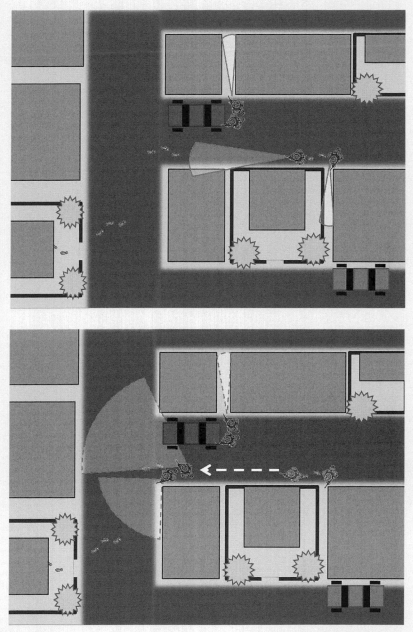

Two 2-man teams cover each other's movement while investigating possible track traps.

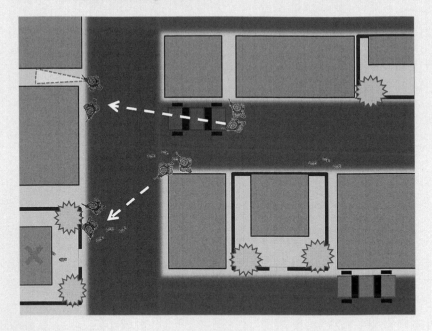

Tracking techniques in an urban environment differ in some cases from those used in a rural setting because the trackers must make bold bounds to check possible track traps. As illustrated, two-man teams bound, covering each other's movement as they search. When one team finds the enemy's sign, it communicates the information back so the rest of the squad and the support group can continue to follow. If the enemy's sign leads to a building, the trackers notify their squad leader, who in turn notifies the support group—which is more capable of conducting a cordon and search of the building and surrounding area.

K-9 TRACKER TEAMS

A K-9 tracker team consists of a scent-tracking dog and its handler. A K-9 team's mission is to establish contact with the enemy by following a scent trail. The team goes through extensive training before it becomes operational. Because of the unique job they perform together and the requirement to establish and maintain a strong bond between the K-9 and the handler, having more than one handler per dog is unacceptable.

A K-9 tracker team used in conjunction with a combat tracker squad can be a great asset if the team's capabilities are understood.

A scent-tracking dog is trained to associate specific tracking commands with specific tracking tasks, and the use of the tracking harness and lead with the requirement to track and find the quarry. It is also trained to identify a specific track scent, follow it until completion of the pursuit, and discriminate the quarry's scent from other contaminating odors along the track line.

A handler is trained to care and groom the dog, conduct kennel maintenance, motivate the dog to follow the quarry's scent trail, and read and interpret the dog's behavior while tracking the quarry.

A dog's sense of smell is vastly superior to that of humans. The dog's ability to recognize different scents and variations shapes its entire existence. The dog can detect even minute microbial disturbances in the environment caused by the quarry's passage. It has the ability to discriminate between thousands of different odors—a highly evolved mechanism that is in large part how the species has been able to sense danger, find food, and survive. The dog's sense of sight is not as good as its sense of smell but it does have good short-range vision and can detect movement rapidly despite being uniformly colorblind. Dogs also have exceptional hearing and are capable of detecting sounds far beyond a human's normal hearing range.

The dog's use of scent is a complex process, and its ability to follow the scent effectively is dependent upon many variables: track age, terrain, climate, training, and the handler. A well-trained and properly conditioned K-9 tracker team can be expected to track the enemy until he is caught or until the scent trail dissipates or is contaminated.

The use of a K-9 tracker team offers both advantages and disadvantages. Initially, a K-9 team may be able to acquire the quarry's track quicker than a visual tracker and speed up the exploitation of an incident site. And a K-9 team may be better able to track over terrain that doesn't capture visual sign well.

A K-9 team can track better during hours of limited visibility than a visual tracker—tracking conditions are better for the team at night because scent will cling to the ground and vegetation in a more concentrated state. And, depending on the handler's ability to read the dog, the dog may alert him that the enemy is near.

As well, a K-9 team is less apt to lose a track when confronted with a contaminated area because it tracks by scent. Once the dog has developed its own scent picture, the enemy cannot be lost except during bad weather or if too much time has passed and the scent has dissipated.

On the other hand, a K-9 tracker team's ability does deteriorate with different weather and climactic conditions. Heat will rapidly evaporate the scent, and strong winds will disperse it, possibly causing the K-9 team to track downwind. Heavy rains will wash the scent trail away. Hard, dry ground will not retain scent because it releases the fewest microbes—it is the most difficult terrain for a K-9 team to track on. The team may also have difficulty following a scent trail on dusty terrain. And strong odors made by other animals can mask the quarry's scent as well as distract the dog. Populated areas may also mask the quarry's scent.

Another disadvantage is that the dog cannot communicate information collected regarding the track picture. The dog is only as good as its handler. Unless the handler is a trained visual tracker, the team will not be able to provide important information learned from the quarry's track picture.

As well, the dog can have a bad day or not want to perform its duties. It will typically tire more quickly than a visual tracker—following the quarry's scent trail is difficult; the level of effort required is so intense that most K-9 teams cannot follow a scent trail for longer than 20 to 30 minutes without resting for 10 to 20 minutes.

WORKING TOGETHER

If a K-9 tracker team is incorporated along with the combat tracker team during the conduct of a combat tracking operation it is imperative that both the squad and the K-9 team know how they will operate with one another. A variety of formations could be used.

The extended line formation with a K-9 team attached is used when terrain is open and there is little or no vegetation to impede visibility. This formation also provides some security for the handler. When security permits, the extended line can speed up the progress of the pursuit.

The wedge formation with K-9 team attached is flexible and easy to control but provides very little frontal security for the dog or handler.

The modified wedge and file formations with a K-9 team attached are used when terrain becomes restrictive and poor visibility occurs between team members, or other factors reduce the team leader's control over his team. They are easy to control but provide very little frontal security for the dog or handler.

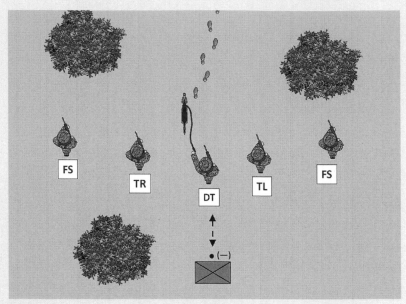

Team extended line formation with a dog team

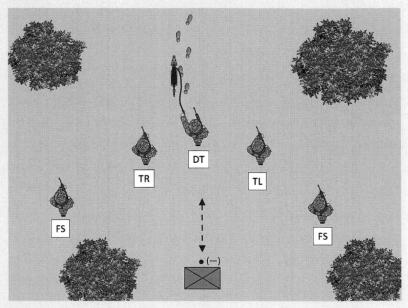

Team wedge formation with a dog team

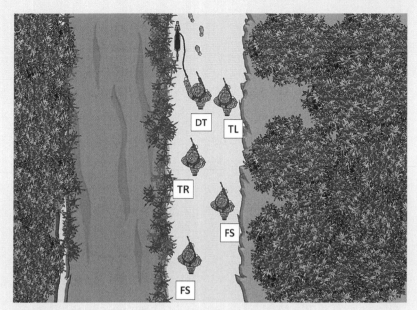

Team modified wedge formation with a dog team

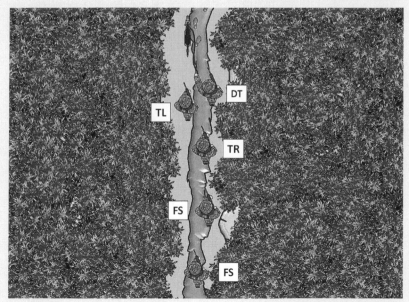

Team file formation with a dog team

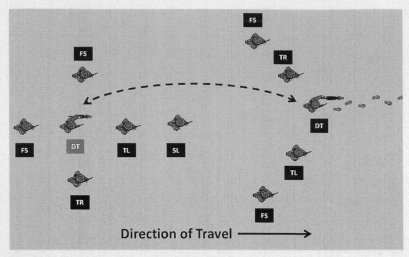

Direction of Travel ———→

Squad column formation with a dog team

When the K-9 tracker team is not employed on a scent trail, it moves to the rear and is incorporated within the trail team's formation until it is called forward to conduct tracking duties.

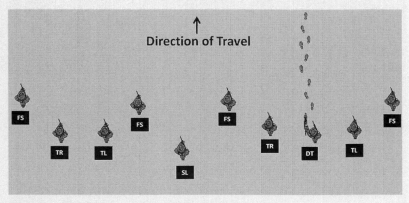

↑
Direction of Travel

Squad line formation with a dog team

The squad line formation provides maximum security and firepower to the front but little security to the flanks. If the K-9 team is following the scent trail, the rest of the combat tracker squad is prepared for likely contact with the enemy.

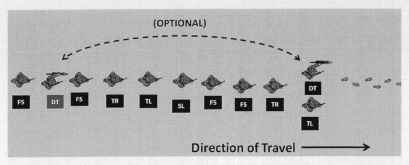

Squad file formation with a dog team

The squad file formation has the same characteristics as the team file. If the K-9 team is following a scent trail, the team is in the lead while the team leader for the lead tracker team provides close-in security. If the K-9 team is not employed on a scent trail, it moves to the rear of the combat tracker squad formation, and squad positioning reverts to an appropriate formation.

ELICITING INFORMATION FROM WITNESSES AND INFORMANTS

When conducting a combat tracking mission and coming into contact with the local population, eliciting information from witnesses and informants can be one of the most reliable and rapid means of obtaining information for immediate use. This information can be exploited immediately and speed up the pursuit operation by providing the trackers with additional information about the movement, position, and activity of the enemy.

Even if the trackers believe the information they have collected is of little or no value, it should still be reported to the TCE. Information that may mean nothing to the trackers on the ground, when compared with other information collected, may provide that important piece of information that now becomes intelligence.

For instance, if the combat trackers follow a track line that comes near or into a village, some of the squad members may be tasked to question the locals about the enemy and their movements. Some locals may be receptive to the patrol and provide firsthand information as witnesses of enemy activity in their area. On the other hand, if the village is uncooperative or evasive the patrol may learn that the village may be either actively supporting or being coerced into supporting the enemy.

ELICITING INFORMATION FROM ENEMY COMBATANTS

At some point the combat trackers may have to conduct tactical questioning of an enemy combatant. Questioning will most likely take place in field conditions after a contact has occurred. Regardless of the situation, time is a critical factor. Questioning should be conducted as soon as possible after a contact and be focused on the trackers' immediate security situation. The first few minutes of capture are usually the most informative when questioning detained enemy personnel. The enemy subject will be confused and the tracker will be able to take advantage of the prisoner's anxiety before he can develop an adequate story.

Information sought through questioning may include the enemy's identity; the locations and number of other enemy forces nearby; the locations of caches of arms, ammunition, and explosives; enemy activities and plans; and booby traps or IEDs in the immediate area that may cause harm to friendly forces.

During the questioning, the tracker must command respect from and dominate his subject. He must be direct, present a professional attitude at all times, and exercise self-control. The tracker conducting the questioning must be alert and quick to detect gaps or contradictions in the subject's story. It is the responsibility of the tracker to create a mood and emotional stimuli that will prompt the subject to tell what he knows. As soon as possible, the prisoner needs to be exfiltrated from the contact site for further questioning by intelligence personnel.

PURSUIT AND ENCIRCLEMENT

Encirclements are an extension of ongoing exploitation or pursuit operations with the goal of isolating and defeating an encircled enemy.

The trackers, along with the support group, apply constant pressure on the fleeing enemy. Concurrently the TCE deploys additional tracker elements to cut for sign in front of the pursuit force and along the quarry's anticipated direction of travel. Mobility is essential when conducting these types of operations. The ability to maneuver multiple elements along the enemy's anticipated direction of travel either by ground or air to close the time and distance gap will be critical.

Encirclement of enemy forces, whether large or small, is the most effective way to completely destroy them. Encirclement operations require enough forces to block all avenues of escape and to attack in force, so they require a relatively large number of troops regardless of the number of enemy involved. If terrain or inadequate forces preclude the effective encirclement of the enemy, then only the most important part of the area is encircled. The planning, preparation, and execution of the operation are aimed at a sudden, complete encirclement that will totally surprise the enemy. Aerial intelligence, surveillance, and reconnaissance (ISR) assets should be used as much as possible to pinpoint the enemy's location and provide constant coverage of the enemy's activities.

All forces employed to conduct the encirclement should reach the line of encirclement simultaneously. The commander of the operation may employ air assets for moving forces to seize critical terrain to accomplish this task. Different enemies will react differently when encircled. Some may become demoralized and offer no resistance; others may react violently on discovering they have been encircled and attempt to break out. The encircling force must be prepared for the enemy's most probable course of action. Should enemy resistance be encountered, friendly forces should respond violently with bold, aggressive action.

"HAMMER AND ANVIL" TECHNIQUE
The hammer and anvil technique employs a stationary blocking force that acts as an "anvil" on one or more sides of the perimeter while the pursuit force uses offensive action as a "hammer" to force the encircled enemy against the blocking force. Depending on the situation, either the "hammer" or the "anvil" can destroy the enemy. Typically it's the pursuit force (the hammer) who will accomplish this task. This method is effective most when the blocking force is located on key terrain that is on or to the rear of a natural obstacle. Once the blocking force is securely established, the destruction of the enemy is conducted methodically, thoroughly, and rapidly. Contact may be initiated by the pursuit force but may also be initiated by attack aviation or indirect fire. It is important that a sudden and swift attack on the enemy's position occur immediately after supporting fire ceases.

After the attack on the enemy, the area is not abandoned immediately but is exploited for hidden enemy personnel and equipment. Enemy documents and records from the objective are collected for intelligence analysis and prisoners are tactically questioned.

ATTACK
When insufficient forces, lack of time, or terrain prevent an encirclement operation, a surprise attack followed by an aggressive pursuit should be employed.

The tracker squad attempts to gain contact without being discovered. If the lead combat tracker squad is discovered by the enemy, the squad conducts the appropriate immediate action drill for the situation. If the enemy attempts to withdraw, the squad opens fire immediately as the tracker support group seeks to envelop the enemy's position. If the enemy attacks, the combat tracker squad immediately conducts the appropriate immediate action drill for the situation. The tracker support group moves forward to the trackers' position, quickly evaluates the situation, and decides on the best course of action to eliminate the enemy. The success or failure of the whole operation depends on the speed and aggressiveness of the combat tracker squad and the speed of the tracker support group in joining the fight to destroy the enemy.

Acknowledgments

It has taken some time to put this book together. At first I started writing it for my own personal use and as time progressed it developed into what it is today. It wasn't till my family and my friends encouraged me to finish this book that it became a reality. I would like to thank Andy Edwards for his great advice and encouragement that helped me forge my manuscript into something that others might want to read.

I would also like to acknowledge Wiley Clark (65th IPCT, 9th ID, RVN, 1968–1969), Mike Landers (CTT-6, 9th ID, RVN, 1967–1968 and 66th IPCT, 25 ID 1968–1970), and Chuck Stewart (61 IPCT, 1st ID, RVN, 1967–1968 and 557th IPCT, 101st ABN DIV, 1970–1971), who contributed valuable information from their own experiences and perspectives as combat trackers during the Vietnam War. I would also like to thank Allen Savory, who was once the commander of the Rhodesian Tracker Combat Unit in Rhodesia. His personal story, although not included in this book, is an amazing tale of a man who lived in what is now Zimbabwe during that nation's insurgency. He is truly a courageous individual.

I also would like to thank my friends: Jason Brokaw for sharing his experiences on a weapons intelligence team in Iraq; and David Diaz, a Special Forces brother, fellow combat tracker, and loyal friend, for his words of encouragement.

Thanks also to my editor Mark Allison, his assistant Kathryn Fulton, and all the people at Stackpole Books who provided me the opportunity to publish this book.

Lastly, I must thank my family, especially my wife Angelique, for all her love, patience, understanding, and endless encouragement.

APPENDIX A

Tire and Tread Tracked Vehicle Impressions

Tire and track impressions are pieces of evidence that retain the distinctive features of a particular vehicle and are visual proof of its passage. Interpretation of these tracks may tell the tracker what type of vehicle made them and possibly how many vehicles passed and in what direction. Evidence of tires or tracks alongside other evidence (footprints, trash, bullet casings, and so on) may help the

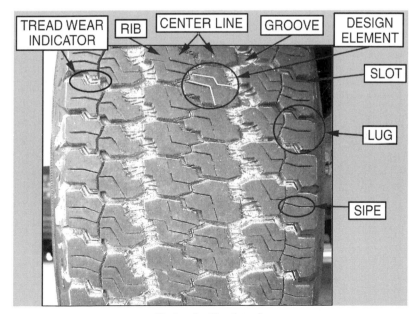

Parts of a tire tread.

tracker determine what happened at a particular incident site and other intelligence about the enemy.

Tire impressions indicate the design of the tread as well as the dimensional features of the individual tires on a specific vehicle. Tire tracks can be used to determine the wheelbase of a vehicle. Tire track evidence consists of:

- track width
- wheelbase dimensions
- turning diameter
- relative positions of turning tracks
- individual tire characteristics such as cuts, scratches, tears, rips, stone holds, nails, plugs and patches, and excessive tread wear.

All tire impressions should be photographed from at least three different angles with and without a scale and measured by length, width, and depth.

MILITARY VEHICLE TRACK AND TIRE TREADS

T-54/55 Medium Battle Tank (Russian)

Type 69 Medium Battle Tank (Chinese)

T-72 Medium Battle Tank (Russian)

PT-76 Amphibious Tank (Russian)

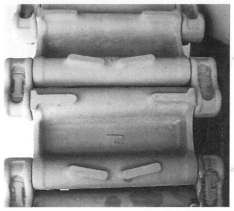

BMP-1 Infantry Combat Vehicle (Russian)

MT-LB Multipurpose Tracked Vehicle (Russian)

AMX-10 Infantry Combat Vehicle (French)

BTR-60 Armored Personnel Carrier (Russian)

Engesa EE 11 Urutu Armored Personnel Carrier (Brazilian)

BRDM-2 Armored Reconnaissance Vehicle (Russian)

122 mm SPH M1974 (2S1) (Russian)

D-20 152 mm Howitzer (Chinese)

100 mm Antitank Gun T-12 (Russian)

PAK 36 Antitank Gun (Russian)

M 1937 45 mm Antitank Gun (Russian)

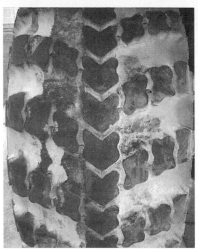

Truck KrAZ 255B (Russian)

Truck W50 LA 3000 kg (German)

UAZ 469 Truck (Russian)

GAZ 69A Truck (Russian)

Truck   Trailer

ZIL 131 Maintenance Truck with Buda Mobile Trailer (Russian)

"Willys" Jeep

S-60 57 mm Automatic Antiaircraft Gun (Chinese)

Type 74 Automatic Antiaircraft Gun (Chinese)

ZPU-4 Automatic Antiaircraft Gun (Russian)

ZPU-2 Automatic Antiaircraft Gun (Russian)

ZPU-1 Automatic Antiaircraft Gun (Russian)

ZU-23 Automatic Antiaircraft Gun (Russian)

Order Formats and Checklists

WARNING ORDER FORMAT

WARNING ORDER _____

References: Refer to higher headquarters' OPORD, and identify map sheet for operation.

Time zone used throughout the order:

Task Organization:

1. **SITUATION.** Find this in higher's OPORD para 1a.
   a. **Area of Interest.** Outline the area of interest on the map.
      (1) Orient relative to each point on the compass (N, S, E, W)
      (2) Box in the entire AO with grid lines
   b. **Area of Operations.** Outline the area of operation on the map. Point out the objective and current location of your unit.
      (1) Trace your zone using boundaries
      (2) Familiarize by identifying natural (terrain) and man-made features in the zone your unit is operating.
   c. **Enemy Forces.** Include significant changes in enemy composition, dispositions, and courses of action. Information not available for inclusion in the initial WARNO can be included in subsequent warning orders (WHO, WHAT, WHERE).

d. **Friendly Forces.** Optional; address only if essential to the WARNO.

(1) Give higher commander's mission (WHO, WHAT, WHEN, WHERE, WHY).

(2) State higher commander's intent.

(3) Point out friendly locations on the map.

e. **Attachments and Detachments.** Give initial task organization, only address major unit changes, and then go to the map board.

2. **MISSION.** Concise statement of the task, and purpose (WHO, WHAT, WHEN, WHERE, WHY). If not all information is known, state which parts of the mission statement are tentative. (STATE MISSION TWICE.)

3. EXECUTION.

a. **Concept of Operations.** Provide as much information as available. The concept should describe the employment of maneuver elements. Give general direction, distance, time of travel, mode of travel, and major tasks to be conducted. Use grids and terrain features. Cover all movements. Specify points where the ground tactical plan starts and stops.

b. **Tasks to Subordinate Units.** Provide specified tasks to subordinate units. Focus on non-tactical instructions for planning and preparation of the operations order. Leaders should also include tactical instructions for executing the mission using control, movement, and AOO for each element in task organization. Planning guidance consists of tasks assigned to elements in the form and order of teams, special teams, and key individuals.

c. **Coordinating Instructions.** Include any information available at that time. If you know it, then at least cover the following items:

- Uniform and equipment common to all.
- Consider the factors of METT-TC and tailor the load for each combat tracker.
- Timeline. (State when, what, where, who and all specified times. Reverse plan. Use ⅓–⅔ rule).
- Give specific priorities in order of completion.
- Give information about coordination meetings.
- Time of OPORD.
- Rehearsals/inspections by priority.
- Earliest movement time.

4. **SUSTAINMENT.** Include any known logistics preparation for the operation.
   a. **Logistics.**
      (1) *Maintenance.* Include weapons and equipment DX time and location.
      (2) Transportation. State method and mode of transportation for infil/exfil. Identify any coordination needed for external assets. Task subordinate leader (if needed) to generate load plan, number of lifts/serials, and bump plan.
      (3) *Supply.* Only include classes of supply that require coordination or special instructions (rations, fuel, ammo, etc.).
   b. **Personnel Services Support.** State any pertinent services for soldiers (religious services, etc.).
   c. **Army Health System Support.** Identify any medical equipment, support, or preventative medicine that needs to be coordinated.

5. **COMMAND AND CONTROL.**
   a. **Command.** Succession of Command. State the succession of command if not covered in the unit's SOP.
   b. **Control.**
      (1) *Command Posts.* Describe the employment of command posts (CPs), including the location of each CP and its

time of opening and closing, as appropriate. Typically, at platoon level the only reference to command posts will be the company CP.

(2) *Reports.* List reports not covered in SOPs.

c. **Signal.** Describe the concept of signal support, including current SOI edition or refer to higher OPORD. Give subordinates guidance on tasks to complete for preparation of the OPORD and the mission. Give time, place, and uniform for the OPORD. Give a time hack and ask for questions.

OPERATION ORDER

[Plans and orders normally contain a code name and are numbered consecutively within a calendar year.]

References: The heading of the plan or order lists maps, charts, data, or other documents the unit will need in order to understand the plan or order. You need not reference the SOP, but may refer to the SOP in the body of the plan or order. Refer to maps by map series number (and country or geographic area, if required), sheet number and name, edition, and scale, if required. "Datum" refers to the mathematical model of the earth that applies to the coordinates on a particular map. It is used to determine coordinates. Different nations use different datum for printing coordinates on their maps. The datum is usually referenced in the marginal information of each map.

Time zone used throughout the order: If the operation will take place in one time zone, use that time zone throughout the order (including annexes and appendixes). If the operation spans several time zones, use Zulu time.

Task organization: Describe the allocation of forces to support the commander's concept. You may show task organization in one of two places: just above paragraph 1, or in an annex, if the task organization is long or complex.

- Go to the map.
- Apply the Orient, Box, Trace, and Familiarize technique to (only) the areas the unit is moving through. (Get this info from the platoon OPORD.)
- Determine the effects of seasonal vegetation within the AO.

1. **SITUATION.**
   a. **Area of Interest.** Describe the area of interest or areas outside of your area of operation that can influence your area of operation.
   b. **Area of Operations.** Describe the area of operations. Refer to the appropriate map and use overlays as needed.
      (1) *Terrain:* Using the OAKOC format, state how the terrain will affect both friendly and enemy forces in the AO. Use the OAKOC from higher's OPORD. Refine it based on your analysis of the terrain in the AO. Follow these steps to brief terrain.
      (2) *Weather.* Describe the aspects of weather that impact operations. Consider the five military aspects of weather to drive your analysis (V,W,T,C,P—Visibility, Winds, Temperature/Humidity, Cloud Cover, Precipitation)

Temp High:	Moonrise:	Sunrise:
Temp Low :	Moonset:	Sunset:
Wind Speed:	Moon Phase:	BMNT:
Wind Direction:	% Illumination:	EENT:

   c. **Enemy Forces.** The enemy situation in higher headquarters' OPORD (paragraph 1c) forms the basis for this. Refine it by adding the detail your subordinates require. Point out on the map the location of recent enemy activity known and suspected.
      (1) State the enemy's composition, disposition, and strength.

(2) Describe his recent activities.

(3) Describe his known or suspected locations and capabilities.

(4) Describe the enemy's most likely and most dangerous course of action.

d. Friendly Forces. Get this information from paragraphs 1d, 2, and 3 of the higher headquarters' OPORD.

(1) Higher Headquarters' Mission and Intent

   (a) Higher Headquarters Two Levels Up

      1. Mission: State the mission of the Higher Unit (2 levels up).

      2. Intent: State intent 2 levels up.

   (b) Higher Headquarters One Level Up

      1. Mission: State the mission of the Higher Unit (1 level up).

      2. Intent: State intent 1 levels up.

(2) *Mission of Adjacent Units.* State locations of units to the left, right, front, and rear. State those units' tasks and purposes; and say how those units will influence yours, particularly adjacent unit patrols.

   (a) Show other units' locations on map board.

   (b) Include statements about the influence each of the above patrols will have on your mission, if any.

   (c) Obtain this information from higher's OPORD. This gives each leader an idea of what other units are doing and where they are going. This information is in paragraph 3b(1) (Execution, Concept of the Operation, Scheme of Movement and Maneuver).

   (d) Also include any information obtained when the leader conducts adjacent unit coordination.

   (e) Attachments and Detachments: Avoid repeating information already listed in Task Organization. Try to put all information in the Task Organization. However, when this information is not in the Task

Organization, list units that are attached or detached to the headquarters that issues the order. State when attachment or detachment will be in effect, if that differs from when the OPORD is in effect such as on order or on commitment of the reserve. Use the term "remains attached" when units will be or have been attached for some time.

2. **MISSION.** State the mission derived during the planning process. A mission statement has no subparagraphs. Answer the 5 W's: Who? What (task)? Where? When? and Why (purpose)?
   - State the mission clearly and concisely. Read it twice.
   - Go to map and point out the exact location of the OBJ and the unit's present location

3. **EXECUTION**
   a. **Commander's Intent.** State the commander's intent, which is his clear, concise statement of what the force must do and the conditions the force must establish with respect to the enemy, terrain, and civil considerations that represent the desired end state.
   b. **Concept of Operations.** Write a clear, concise concept statement. Describe how the unit will accomplish its mission from start to finish. Base the number of subparagraphs, if any, on what you consider appropriate, the level of leadership, and the complexity of the operation.
   c. **Scheme of Movement and Maneuver.** Describe the employment of maneuver units in accordance with the concept of operations. Address subordinate units and attachments by name. State each one's mission as a task and purpose. Ensure that the subordinate units' missions support that of the main effort. Focus on actions on the objective. Include a detailed plan and criteria for engagement/ disengagement, an alternate plan in case of compromise or

unplanned enemy force movement, and a withdrawal plan. The brief is to be sequential, taking you from start to finish, covering all aspects of the operation.
- Brief from the start of your operation to mission complete.
- Cover all routes, primary and alternate, from insertion, through AOO, to link-up, until mission complete.
- Brief your plan for crossing known danger areas.
- Brief your plan for reacting to enemy contact.
- Brief any approved targets/CCPs as you brief your routes.

d. **Scheme of Fires.** State scheme of fires to support the overall concept and state who (which maneuver unit) has priority of fire. You can use the PLOT-CR format (Purpose, Location, Observer, Trigger, Communication method, Resources) to plan fires. Refer to the target list worksheet and overlay here, if applicable. Discuss specific targets and point them out on the terrain model.

e. **Casualty Evacuation.** Provide a detailed CASEVAC plan during each phase of the operation. Include CCP locations, tentative extraction points, and methods of extraction.

f. **Tasks to Subordinate Units.** Clearly state the missions or tasks for each subordinate unit that reports directly to the headquarters issuing the order. List the units in the task organization, including reserves. Use a separate subparagraph for each subordinate unit. State only the tasks needed for comprehension, clarity, and emphasis. Place tactical tasks that affect two or more units in Coordinating Instructions (subparagraph 3h). Platoon leaders may task their subordinate squads to provide any of the following special teams: reconnaissance and security, assault, support, aid and litter, EPW and search, clearing, and demolitions. You may also include detailed instructions for the platoon sergeant, RTO, compass man, and pace man.

h. Coordinating Instructions. This is always the last subparagraph under paragraph 3. List only the instructions that apply to two or more units, and which are seldom covered in unit SOPs. Refer the user to an annex for more complex instructions. The information listed below is required.

(1) *Time Schedule.* State time, place, uniform, and priority of rehearsals, backbriefs, inspections, and movement.

(2) *Commander's Critical Information Requirements.* Include PIR and FFIR

   (a) Priority intelligence requirements. PIR includes all intelligence that the commander must have for planning and decision making.

   (b) Friendly force information requirements. FFIR include what the commander needs to know about friendly forces available for the operation. It can include personnel status, ammunition status, and leadership capabilities.

(3) *Essential Elements of Friendly Information.* EEFI are critical aspects of friendly operations that, if known by the enemy, would compromise, lead to failure, or limit success of the operation.

(4) *Risk-Reduction Control Measures.* These are measures unique to the operation. They supplement the unit SOP and can include mission-oriented protective posture, operational exposure guidance, vehicle recognition signals, and fratricide prevention measures.

(5) *Rules of Engagement (ROE).*

(6) *Environmental Considerations.*

(7) *Force Protection.*

4. SUSTAINMENT. Describe the concept of sustainment, including logistics, personnel, and medical.

a. Logistics.

(1) *Sustainment Overlay.* Include current and proposed company trains locations, CCPs (include marking method),

equipment collection points, HLZs, AXPs, and any friendly sustainment locations (FOBs, COPs etc).

(2) *Maintenance.* Include weapons and equipment DX time and location.

(3) *Transportation.* State method and mode of transportation for infil/exfil, load plan, number of lifts/serials, bump plan, recovery assets, recovery plan.

(4) *Supply.*

Class I—Rations plan.

Class III—Petroleum.

Class V—Ammunition.

Class VII—Major end items.

Class VIII—Medical.

Class IX—Repair parts.

Distribution Methods.

(5) *Field Services.* Include any services provided or required (laundry, showers, etc.).

b. Personnel Services Support.

(1) Method of marking and handling EPWs.

(2) Religious Services.

c. Army Health System Support.

(1) *Medical Command and Control.* Include location of medics and identify medical leadership, personnel controlling medics, and method of marking patients.

(2) *Medical Treatment.* State how wounded or injured soldiers will be treated (self aid, buddy aid, CLS, EMT, etc.).

(3) *Medical Evacuation.* Describe how dead or wounded, friendly and enemy personnel will be evacuated and identify aid and litter teams. Include special equipment needed for evacuation.

(4) *Preventive Medicine.* Identify any preventive medicine soldiers may need for the mission (sunblock, chapstick, insect repellant, in-country specific medicine, etc.).

5. **COMMAND AND CONTROL.** State where command and control facilities and key leaders are located during the operation.

  a. Command.

  (1) *Location of Commander/Patrol Leader.* State where the commander intends to be during the operation, by phase if the operation is phased.

  (2) *Succession of Command.* State the succession of command if not covered in the unit's SOP.

  b. Control.

  (1) *Command Posts.* Describe the employment of command posts (CPs), including the location of each CP and its time of opening and closing, as appropriate. Typically at platoon level the only reference to command posts will be the company CP.

  (2) *Reports.* List reports not covered in SOPs.

  c. Signal. Describe the concept of signal support, including current SOI edition, or refer to higher OPORD.

  (1) Identify the SOI index that is in effect.

  (2) Identify methods of communication by priority.

  (3) Describe pyrotechnics and signals, including arm and hand signals (demonstrate).

  (4) Give code words such as OPSKEDs.

  (5) Give challenge and password (use behind friendly lines).

  (6) Give number combination (use forward of friendly lines).

  (7) Give running password.

  (8) Give recognition signals (near/far and day/night).

Actions after Issuance of OPORD:

- Issue annexes
- Highlight next hard time
- Give time hack
- Ask for questions

FRAGMENTARY ORDER

A FRAGO is an abbreviated form of an operation order, usually issued daily, which eliminates the need for restating portions of the OPORD. It is issued after an OPORD to change or modify that order or to execute a branch or sequel to that order.

FRAGMENTARY ORDER_____

Time zone referenced throughout order:

Task organization:

1. **SITUATION** [Brief only the changes from base OPORD specific to this operation]
   a. **Area of Interest.** State any changes to the area of interest.
   b. **Area of Operations.** State any changes to the area of operations.
      (1) Terrain [Note any changes that will effect operation in new area of operations]: observation/fields of fire, cover and concealment, obstacles, key terrain, and avenues of approach.
      (2) Weather and light data:

Temp High:	Moonrise:	Sunrise:
Temp Low :	Moonset:	Sunset:
Wind Speed:	Moon Phase:	BMNT:
Wind Direction:	% Illumination:	EENT:
Forecast:		

   c. **Enemy.**
      (1) Composition, disposition, and strength.
      (2) Capabilities.
      (3) Recent activities.
      (4) Most likely COA.

d. Friendly.
   (1) Higher mission.
   (2) Adjacent patrols task/purpose.
   (3) Adjacent patrol objective/route (if known).

2. **MISSION** (Who, what [task], when, where, why [purpose]—from higher HQ maneuver paragraph).

3. **EXECUTION**
   a. Commander's Intent. Include any changes or state "No Change."
   b. Concept of Operations. Include any changes or state "No Change."
   c. Scheme of Movement and Maneuver. Include any changes or state "No Change."
   d. Scheme of Fires. Include any changes or state "No Change."
   e. Casualty Evacuation. Include any changes or state "No Change."
   f. Tasks to Subordinate Units. Include any changes or state "No Change."
   h. Coordinating Instructions. Include any changes or state "No Change."
     (1) Time Schedule.
     (2) Commander's Critical Information Requirements.
        (a) Priority intelligence requirements.
        (b) Friendly force information requirements.
     (3) Essential elements of friendly information.
     (4) Risk-Reduction Control Measures.
     (5) Rules of Engagement (ROE).
     (6) Environmental Considerations.
     (7) Force Protection.

4. SUSTAINMENT. Only cover changes from base order—use standard format and items that have not changed should be briefed "no change."

a. Logistics.

(1) Sustainment Overlay.

(2) Maintenance.

(3) Transportation.

(4) Supply.

Class I:

Class III:

Class V:

Class VII:

Class VIII:

Class IX:

Distribution Methods:

(5) Field Services.

b. Personnel Services Support.

(1) Method of marking and handling EPWs.

(2) Religious Services.

c. Army Health System Support.

(1) Medical Command and Control.

(2) Medical Treatment.

(3) Medical Evacuation.

(4) Preventive Medicine.

5. COMMAND AND CONTROL. Only brief changes to base order. If there are changes, state where command and control facilities and key leaders are located during the operation.

a. Command.

(1) *Location of Commander/Patrol Leader.* State where the commander intends to be during the operation, by phase if the operation is phased.

(2) *Succession of Command.* State the succession of command if not covered in the unit's SOP.

b. Control.

(1) *Command Posts.* Describe the employment of command posts (CPs), including the location of each CP and its time of opening and closing, as appropriate. Typically at platoon level the only reference to command posts will be the company CP.

(2) *Reports.* List reports not covered in SOPs.

c. Signal. Describe the concept of signal support, including current SOI edition, or refer to higher OPORD.

(1) Identify the SOI index that is in effect.

(2) Identify methods of communication by priority.

(3) Describe pyrotechnics and signals, including arm and hand signals (demonstrate).

(4) Give code words such as OPSKEDs.

(5) Give challenge and password (use behind friendly lines).

(6) Give number combination (use forward of friendly lines).

(7) Give running password.

(8) Give recognition signals (near/far and day/night).

COORDINATION CHECKLISTS

The following checklists are items that a leader must check when planning for an operation. In some cases, he will coordinate directly with the appropriate staff section; in most cases this information will be provided by the commander.

INTELLIGENCE COORDINATION CHECKLIST

The unit one level higher constantly updates intelligence. This ensures that the platoon leader's plan reflects the most recent enemy activity.

1. Identification of enemy unit.
2. Weather and light data.

3. Terrain update.
   a. Aerial photos.
   b. Trails and obstacles not on map.
4. Known or suspected enemy locations.
5. Weapons.
6. Probable course of action.
7. Recent enemy activities.
8. Reaction time of reaction forces.
9. Civilians on the battlefield.
10. Update to CCIR.

OPERATIONS COORDINATION CHECKLIST
The squad leader coordinates with the company commander/
platoon leader to confirm the mission and operational plan, receive
last-minute changes, and either update subordinates in person or
issue a FRAGO:
1. Mission backbrief.
2. Identification of friendly units.
3. Changes in the friendly situation.
4. Route selection, LZ/PZ/DZ selection.
5. Linkup procedures.
   a. Contingencies
   b. QRF
   c. QRF Frequency
6. Transportation/movement plan.
7. Resupply (with S-4).
8. Signal plan.
9. Departure and reentry of forward units.
10. Special equipment requirements.
11. Adjacent units in the area of operations.
12. Rehearsal areas.
13. Method of insertion/extraction.

FIRE SUPPORT COORDINATION CHECKLIST
The squad leader coordinates the following with the forward observer (FO):
1. Mission backbrief.
2. Identification of supporting unit.
3. Mission and objective.
4. Route to and from the objective (include alternate routes).
5. Time of departure and expected time of return.
6. Unit target list (from fire plan).
7. Type of available support (artillery, mortar, naval gunfire, and aerial support, including Army, Navy, and Air Force) and their locations.
8. Ammunition available (including different fuses).
9. Priority of fires.
10. Control measures.
   a. Checkpoints.
   b. Boundaries.
   c. Phase lines.
   d. Fire support coordination measures.
   e. Priority targets (target list).
   f. RFA (restrictive fire area).
   g. RFL (restrictive fire line).
   h. NFA (no-fire area).
   i. Precoordinated authentication.
11. Communication (include primary and alternate means, emergency signals, and code words).

COORDINATION WITH FORWARD UNIT CHECKLIST
A squad that requires foot movement through a friendly forward unit must coordinate with that unit's commander for a safe and orderly passage. If no time and place has been designated for coordination with the forward unit, the platoon/squad leader should set a time and place to coordinate with the S-3. He must talk with

someone at the forward unit who has the authority to commit the forward unit to assist the platoon/squad during departure. Coordination is a two-way exchange of information.

1. Identification (yourself and your unit).
2. Size of patrol.
3. Time(s) and place(s) of departure and return, location(s) of departure point(s), ERRP, and de-trucking points.
4. General area of operations.
5. Information on terrain and vegetation.
6. Known or suspected enemy positions or obstacles.
7. Possible enemy ambush sites.
8. Latest enemy activity.
9. Detailed information on friendly positions such as crew-served weapons, FPF.
10. Fire and barrier plan.
    a. Support the unit can furnish. What can they do and for how long?
       (1) Fire support.
       (2) Litter teams.
       (3) Navigational signals and aids.
       (4) Guides.
       (5) Communications.
       (6) Reaction units.
       (7) Other.
    b. Call signs and frequencies.
    c. Pyrotechnic plan.
    d. Challenge and password, running password, number combination.
    e. Emergency signals and code words.
    f. If the unit is relieved, pass the information to the relieving unit.
    g. Recognition signals.

ADJACENT UNIT COORDINATION CHECKLIST

Immediately after the OPORD or mission briefing, the squad leader should check with other leaders who will be operating in the same areas. If the leader is unaware of any other units operating is his area, he should check with the S-3 during the operations coordination. The S-3 can help arrange this coordination if necessary. The squad leaders should exchange the following information with other units operating in the same area:

1. Identification of the unit.
2. Mission and size of unit.
3. Planned times and points of departure and reentry.
4. Route(s).
5. Fire support and control measures.
6. Frequencies and call signs.
7. Challenge and password, running password, number combination.
8. Pyrotechnic plan.
9. Any information that the unit may have about the enemy.
10. Recognition signals.

REHEARSAL AREA COORDINATION CHECKLIST

The assistant patrol leader coordinates the use of the rehearsal area to facilitate the unit's safe, efficient, and effective use of the rehearsal area before its mission:

1. Identification of your unit.
2. Mission.
3. Terrain similar to objective site.
4. Security of the area.
5. Availability of aggressors.
6. Use of blanks, pyrotechnics, and ammunition.
7. Mock-ups available.
8. Time the area is available (preferably when light conditions approximate light conditions of patrol).
9. Transportation.
10. Coordination with other units using the area.

ARMY AVIATION COORDINATION CHECKLIST
The patrol leader coordinates this with the company commander or
S-3 Air to facilitate the time and detailed and effective use of avia-
tion assets as they apply to the tactical mission:

1. SITUATION.
   a. Enemy.
      (1) Air capability.
      (2) ADA capability.
      (3) Include in weather: percent illum, illum angle, NVG
          window, ceiling, and visibility.
   b. Friendly.
      (1) Unit(s) supporting operation, axis of movement/corri-
          dor/routes.
      (2) ADA status.
2. MISSION.
3. EXECUTION.
   a. Concept of the Operation. Overview of what requesting unit
      wants to accomplish with the air assault/air movement.
   b. Tasks to Combat Units.
      (1) Infantry.
      (2) Attack aviation.
   c. Tasks to Combat Support Units.
      (1) Artillery.
      (2) Aviation (lift).
   d. Coordinating Instructions.
      (1) Pickup Zone.
          • Direction of landing.
          • Time of landing/ flight direction.
          • Locations of PZ and alternate PZ.
          • Loading procedures.
          • Marking of PZ (panel, smoke, SM, lights).
          • Flight route planned (SP, ACP, RP).
          • Formations: PZ, en route, LZ.

- Code words:
  - —PZ secure (before landing), PZ clear (lead bird and last bird).
  - —Alternate PZ (at PZ, en route, LZ), names of PZ/alt PZ.
- TAC air/ artillery.
- Number of pax per bird and for entire lift.
- Equipment carried by individuals.
- Marking of key leaders.
- Abort criteria (PZ, en route, LZ).

(2) Landing Zone.
- Direction of landing.
- False insertion plans.
- Time of landing (LZ time).
- Locations of LZ and alt LZ.
- Marking of LZ (panel, smoke, SM, lights).
- Formation of landing.
- Code words, LZ name, alternate LZ name.
- TAC air/artillery preparation, and fire support coordination.
- Secure LZ or not?

4. SUSTAINMENT. Only brief specifics not covered in base order to include number of aircraft per lift and number of lifts, whether the aircraft will refuel/rearm during mission, special equipment carried by personnel, aircraft configuration, and bump plan.

a. Logistics.
(1) Sustainment overlay.
(2) Maintenance.
(3) Transportation.
(4) Supply.
> Class I:
> Class III:
> Class V:
> Class VII:

Class VIII:

Class IX:

Distribution methods:

(5) Field services.

b. Personnel Services Support.

(1) Method of marking and handling EPWs.

(2) Religious services.

c. Army Health System Support.

(1) Medical command and control.

(2) Medical treatment.

(3) Medical evacuation.

(4) Preventive medicine.

5. COMMAND AND CONTROL.

a. Command.

(1) *Location of Commander/Patrol Leader.* State where the commander intends to be during the operation, by phase if the operation is phased. Also include locations of air missions commander, ground tactical commander, and air assault task force commander.

(2) *Succession of Command.* State the succession of command if not covered in the unit's SOP.

b. Control.

(1) *Command Posts.* Describe the employment of command posts (CPs), including the location of each CP and its time of opening and closing, as appropriate. Typically, at platoon level the only reference to command posts will be the company CP.

(2) *Reports.* List reports not covered in SOPs.

c. Signal. Describe the concept of signal support, including current SOI edition, or refer to higher OPORD.

(1) Identify the SOI index that is in effect.

(2) Identify methods of communication by priority.

(3) Describe pyrotechnics and signals, including arm and hand signals (demonstrate).

(4) Give code words such as OPSKEDs.

(5) Give challenge and password (use behind friendly lines).
(6) Give number combination (use forward of friendly lines).
(7) Give running password.
(8) Give recognition signals (near/far and day/night).

VEHICULAR MOVEMENT COORDINATION CHECKLIST
The platoon sergeant or first sergeant coordinates this with the supporting unit to facilitate the effective, detailed, and efficient use of vehicular support and assets:
  1. Identification of the unit.
  2. Supporting unit identification.
  3. Number and type of vehicles and tactical preparation.
  4. En-trucking point.
  5. Departure time.
  6. Preparation of vehicles for movement.
     a. Driver responsibilities.
     b. Platoon/squad responsibilities.
  c. Special supplies/equipment required.
  7. Availability of vehicles for preparation/rehearsals/inspection (times and locations).
  8. Routes.
     a. Primary.
     b. Alternate.
     c. Checkpoints.
  9. De-trucking points.
     a. Primary.
     b. Alternate.
  10. Order of march.
  11. Speed.
  12. Emergency procedures and signals.

APPENDIX C

Mission Debrief Format

THE MISSION DEBRIEF

UNIT DESIGNATION: _____

MISSION NUMBER: _____

DTG OF DEPARTURE: _____

DTG OF RETURN: _____

MAPS USED:

Name:	Scale:	Edition:	Series:	Sheet #:
1.				
2.				
3.				

A. SIZE AND COMPOSITION OF UNIT.
   1. Organization:
   2. Patrol personnel:
   3. Equipment:
   4. Individual small arms:
   5. Alternate or crew-served weapons:
   6. Mines:

    7. Grenades:

    8. Booby-traps:

    9. Demolitions:

  10. Special weapons:

  11. FM radios (VHF):

  12. HF radios:

  13. Smoke grenades:

  14. VS-17 panels:

  15. Strobe lights:

  16. Pen flares:

  17. Compasses and GPSs:

  18. Flashlights:

  19. Individual items:

  20. Optical equipment:

  21. Maps:

  22. Photographic equipment:

B. MISSION: (As per operations order)

C. INTELLIGENCE REQUIREMENTS:

D. SUMMARY:

E. SUSPECT(S):

F. EVIDENCE:

G. ADDITIONAL INFORMATION:

H. INFILTRATION:
    1. Method of infiltration:
    2. Point of departure:

I. THREAT FORCES OBSERVED EN ROUTE:
 1. Ground activity:
 2. Air activity:
 3. Miscellaneous activity:

J. ROUTES IN: (Unit provides a detailed description, written and overlay, of routes from assembly area to objective.)
 1. Planned primary and alternate routes:
 2. Actual routes taken and reason for deviation from planned routes:
 3. Routes followed:
 4. Halts en route, to include security and objective:
 5. DTG arrived at objective area:

K. TERRAIN:
 1. Land forms:
 2. Vegetation:
  a. Lowland:
   (1) Thickness:
   (2) Undergrowth:
   (3) Effects on maneuverability of vehicles and dismounted soldiers:
   (4) Thickness of overhead cover:
  b. Ridge and mountainsides:
   (1) Thickness:
   (2) Undergrowth:
   (3) Effects on maneuverability of vehicles and dismounted soldiers:
   (4) Thickness of overhead cover:
  c. High ground, ridgetops and hilltops:
   (1) Thickness:
   (2) Undergrowth:

      (3) Effects on maneuverability of vehicles and dis-
mounted soldiers:

      (4) Thickness of overhead cover:

  d. Key terrain:

  e. Restrictive terrain:

  f. Major obstacles to vehicles and soldiers:

  g. Availability of cover and concealment:

  h. Major avenues of approach (any that an attacking element battalion-size or larger could maneuver through):

3. Roads, trails, railroad tracks:

  a. Type (single- or multilane, hard, gravel, or dirt surface):

  b. Condition (dry, wet, muddy, well-used, seldom used):

  c. Trafficability (types of vehicle terrain will support):

  d. Trails or roads not on the map:

  e. What was the condition of the trails followed?

  f. Did the trails show signs of recent use?

  g. Bypasses and/or alternate routes:

4. All open areas:

  a. Type (pasture, cultivated, new tree farm):

  b. Suitability for use as a PZ, LZ, or DZ:

  c. Will the ground support tracked or wheeled vehicles?

5. Rivers, streams, and lakes:

  a. Location:

  b. Length:

  c. Width:

  d. Depth:

  e. Current (speed and direction):

  f. Slopes of the bank:

  g. Composition of the soil on the bottom of the banks:

  h. Dimensions of the dry bed:

  i. Navigability of large streams:

  j. Fordability to vehicles and soldiers:

    k. Bridges (classification report):

    l. Trafficability under the bridge for boats or barges:

L. SOIL:

    1. Appearance (color):

    2. Composition (clay, sand, rocky, etc.):

    3. Hardness (dry, wet, muddy, etc.):

    4. Ease of digging:

    5. Any standing water?

M. TRAILS:

    1. Location and direction:

    2. Width:

    3. Estimated use (by humans or animals):

    4. Overhead canopy:

    5. Undergrowth along sides of trails:

    6. Direction signs, symbols, or target indicators on the trail:

    7. Surface characteristics (hard packed, soft earth or dead vegetation):

    8. Description of vehicle tracks:

N. ROADS:

    1. Location and direction (in degrees):

    2. Width (in meters):

    3. Surface material (sand, packed earth, gravel, asphalt, concrete, etc.):

    4. Indicators of movement on the road:

    5. Road maintenance (craters repaired, potholes, etc.):

    6. Road drainage characteristics:

    7. Obstructions:

    8. Road signs, markers, etc.:

    9. Description of vehicle tracks (if applicable):

O. MAP CORRECTIONS (roads, streams, built-up areas, etc.):

P. OBSERVATIONS OF CIVILIAN ACTIVITY:
1. When and where were people seen?
2. How many people were observed?
3. What was their physical condition?
4. Were they friendly?
5. What were the people doing?
6. Ethnic and tribal affiliation?
7. What kind of clothing were they wearing? (Color and condition of clothing, footwear and headwear).
8. What information did they provide?
9. Influence of political groups?
10. Influence of chiefs/village elders?
11. Influence of religious or spiritual mediums?

Q. OBSERVATIONS OF STRUCTURES AND OTHER MANMADE OBJECTS:
1. Location(s):
2. Quantity:
3. Shape(s), size(s) and purpose(s):
4. Construction materials:
5. Markings:
6. Contents of structure:
7. Estimated time of last use:
8. Indications of occupancy:
9. Animals or animal pens in the vicinity:
10. Crops in the vicinity:
    a. Type:
    b. Size of field or paddy:
    c. Care of the area:
    d. Stage of development:
    e. Food and water storage area(s):

R. ENEMY HIDES OR CAMPS FOUND:
   1. Grid reference?
   2. Was it occupied?
   3. If so, by how many?
   4. If not, how long had it been evacuated?
   5. Number of shelters and estimated number of occupants:
   6. Temporary or permanent installations or structures?
   7. Trenches, fighting positions, bunkers, or advanced warning positions (location, size, number, and description of each):
      a. Stage of development:
      b. Efforts to conceal from aerial view:
   8. Any sentry posts? If so, how were they spotted?
   9. Any warning signals or booby traps?
   10. Entry and exit points?
   11. Any food and water storage in or near the camp?
   12. Any weapons or ammunition found?
   13. If so, what condition and quantity?
   14. Were there any radio or press equipment?
   15. Were there any documents found? If so, what:
   16. Where were they found?
   17. Any indication of direction taken by the enemy when escaping the camp?

S. SURVEILLANCE OF ENEMY:
   1. How does the enemy employ counterreconnaissance assets?
   2. Was the patrol tracked at any time?
   3. Enemy discipline:
   4. Does the enemy appear well trained?
   5. What type of equipment is the enemy using?

T. ENEMY CONTACTS:
   1. Where was contact made?
   2. How many were there?

3. What was the enemy's reaction time if contact was made?
4. How were they dressed? If in uniform, give details.
5. What was the condition of their weapons?
6. Estimate of quantity of ammunition.
7. Any indication that could lead to the identification of the leader?
8. How were orders given and how was control maintained?
9. Were any formations used in the:
   a. Attack?
   b. Defense?
   c. Snipers?
10. Any automatic weapons or crew-served weapons used?
11. Did the enemy appear healthy?
12. What was their morale like?
13. What language was spoken?
14. What system did the enemy use for signalling (including the use of radios)?
15. Casualties:
    a. Friendly?
    b. Enemy?
16. Any captured enemy?
17. Any enemy surrender?
18. Have the enemy dead been identified? If not, were photos taken?
19. Were there any recognizable identification marks?
20. When was contact broken?
21. In which direction did the enemy escape?
22. Did they use known trails?
23. Where was the patrol when the enemy tracks could no longer be followed?

U. ROUTES BACK:
    1. Planned primary and alternate routes:
    2. Actual routes taken and reason for deviation from planned routes:

3. Halts en route, including security and linkup with vehicle:
4. DTG arrived at assembly area:

V. EXFILTRATION:
1. DTG of exfiltration:
2. Method of exfiltration:
3. Point of exfiltration:

W. TIME AND POINT OF RETURN:

X. CONDITION OF UNIT:
1. Disposition of dead and wounded personnel:
2. Unit leader's estimate of when unit will be ready to start a new mission:
3. Personnel and equipment shortages:

Y. ITEMS OF POTENTIAL TACTICAL VALUE:
1. Were all maps and any other identifiable material returned with the unit?
2. If not, what is missing? (State item and approximately where lost.)

Z. CONCLUSIONS AND RECOMMENDATIONS:
1. To what extent was the mission accomplished?
2. Recommended changes in tactics or procedures:
3. What additional information is needed in the OPORD?
4. Recommended equipment changes:
5. Effects of weather on unit's operational capability:
   a. Visibility:
   b. Cloud cover:
   c. Rainfall:
   d. Ground fog:
   e. Winds:
   f. Temperatures and humidity:
   g. Illumination at night:

6. What else should another unit know before going into this area?
7. Additional areas or information that has not been covered. Is there something that should be highlighted?

UNIT LEADER (Print name and grade): _____
_____

UNIT:_____SIGNATURE:_____

DEBRIEFER (Print name and grade): _____
_____

UNIT:_____SIGNATURE:_____

ADDITIONAL REMARKS BY DEBRIEFER:

ENCLOSURES:
Patrol log
Communications log
Surveillance log
Photograph log

APPENDIX D

Fire Support

Planning is the continual process of selecting targets on which fires are prearranged to support a phase of the commander's plan.

PRINCIPLES
1. Consider what the commander wants to do.
2. Plan early and continuously.
3. Exploit all available targeting assets.
4. Use all available lethal and nonlethal fire support means.
5. Use the lowest echelon able to furnish effective support.
6. Observe all fires.
7. Use the most effective fire support asset available.
8. Provide adequate fire support.
9. Avoid unnecessary duplication.
10. Provide for safety of friendly forces and installations.
11. Provide for flexibility.
12. Furnish the type of fire support requested.
13. Consider the airspace.
14. Provide rapid and effective coordination.
15. Keep all fire support informed.

FIRE SUPPORT TASKS
ALL OPERATIONS
1. Locate targets.
2. Integrate all available assets.

3. Destroy, neutralize, or suppress all enemy direct and indirect fire systems.
4. Provide illumination and smoke.
5. Provide fires in support of JAAT and SEAD missions.
6. Deliver scatterable mines.
7. Prepare for future operations.
8. Provide positive clearance of fires.

OFFENSIVE OPERATIONS
1. Support the movement to contact, chance contact.
2. Soften enemy defenses before the attack by arranging short, violent preparations, where required.
3. Provide support during the attack by attacking high payoff targets.
4. Plan for deep and flanking fires.
5. Plan fires during consolidation.
6. Provide counter-fires.

CAPABILITIES

FIELD ARTILLERY

Weapon	Max Range (m)	Min Range (m)	Max Rate (Rnds per Min)	Burst Radius	Sustained Rate (Rnds per Min)
105mm Howitzer M102, Towed	11,500 14,500 (RAP)	0	10 for 3 min	35 m	3
105mm Howitzer M119, Towed	14,000m	0	6 for 2 min	35 m	3 rds for 30 min, then 1 rd per min
155mm Howitzer M198, Towed	18,100 30,000 (RAP)	0	4 for 3 min 2 for 30 min	50 m	1 rd per min Temp Dependent
155mm Howitzer M109A2/A3 SP	18,100 23,500 (RAP)	0	4 for 3 min	50 m	1 for 60 min 0.5
203mm Howitzer M110A2, SP	22,900 30,000 (RAP)	0	1.5 for 3 min	80 m	0.5

MORTARS

Weapon	Munition Available	Max Range (m)	Min Range (m)	Max Rate (Rnds per Min)	Burst Radius	Sustained Rate (Rnds per Min)
60mm	HE,WP,ILLUM	3500 (HE)	70 (HE)	30 for 4 min	30 m	20
81mm	HE,WP,ILLUM	4790 (HE)	70 (HE)	25 for 2 min	38 m	8
107mm	HE,WP,ILLUM	6840 (HE)	770 (HE)	18 for 1 min 9 for 5 min	40 m	3
120mm	HE,SMK,ILLUM	7,200 (HE)	180 (HE)	15 for 1 min	60 m	5

NAVAL GUNS

Weapon	Full Charge	Reduced Charge	Max Rate (Rnds per Min)	Sustained Rate (Rnds per Min)
5 in / 38	15,904	8,114	20	15
5 in / 54	23,133	12,215	35	20
16 in / 50	36,188	22,951	2	1

DANGER CLOSE

The term "DANGER CLOSE" is included in the "method of engagement" portion of the call for fire when the target is within 600 meters of any friendly troops for both mortars and field artillery. When adjusting naval gunfire the term "DANGER CLOSE" is announced when the target is located within 750 meters when using 5 inch or smaller naval guns. For naval guns larger than 5 inch, "DANGER CLOSE" is announced when the target is within 1000 meters.

The creeping method of adjustment is used exclusively during "DANGER CLOSE" missions. The FO should make range changes by creeping the rounds to the target using corrections of no more than 100 meters.

TARGET OVERLAY

A complete fire support overlay must include:
1. Unit and official capacity of person making overlay.
2. Date the overlay was prepared.
3. Map sheet number.
4. Effective period of overlay (DTG).
5. Priority target.
6. ORP location.
7. Call signs and frequencies. (PRI/ALT)
8. Routes—primary/alternate.
9. Phase lines/checkpoints used by the patrol.
10. Spares.
11. Index marks to position overlay on map.
12. Objective.
13. Target symbols.
14. Description, location and remarks column, complete.

Sterile Overlay must include:
1. Index marks to position overlay on map.
2. Target symbols.

TARGET OVERLAY SYMBOLS
1. Point Target

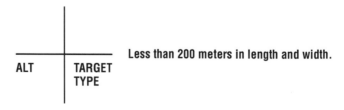

Less than 200 meters in length and width.

ALT   **TARGET TYPE**

2. Linear Target:

Target #

More than 200 meters but less than 600 meters long.

3. Circular Target:

Target #   Undisclosed area and desired radius.

CLOSE AIR SUPPORT (CAS)

There are two types of close air support requests, planned and immediate. Planned request are processed by the Army chain to Corps for approval. Immediate requests are initiated at any level and processed by the battalion S-3 FSO, and Air Liaison Officer.

Format for requesting immediate CAS:
1. Observer identification.
2. Warning order (Request Close Air)
3. Target location (Grid).
4. Target description. (Description must include, as a minimum: type and number of targets; activity or movement; point or area targets; include desired results on target and time on target.)
5. Location of friendly forces
6. NAV details (Elevation).
7. Threats—ADA, small arms, etc.
8. Hazards—friendly aircraft in area.
9. Wind direction.

CLOSE AIR SUPPORT CAPABILITIES

CLOSE AIR SUPPORT RESOURCES

Aircraft	Service	Characteristics
A-4*	N/MC	Subsonic; typical load 4000 lbs, maximum load 9000 lbs.
A-7*	AF Res/NG/N	Very accurate delivery; subsonic; typical load 8000 lbs, max load 15,000 lbs.
A-10*	AF	Specialized CAS aircraft; subsonic; typical load 6000 lbs, max load 16,000 lbs; 30mm gun.
F-16*	AF	A multi-role aircraft; complements the F-4 and F-15 in an air-to-air role. Most accurate ground delivery system in the inventory; supersonic; typical load 6000 lbs, max load 10,600 lbs.
F-18*	N/MC	A multi-role fighter scheduled to replace the F-4. A wide variety of air-to-surface weapons. Typical load 7000 lbs, max load 17,000 lbs, 20mm gun mounted in the nose; air-to-air missiles.
AC-130	AF/R	A specialized CAS/RACO aircraft, propeller driven. Two models: A model is equipped with two 40mm guns, two 20mm guns and two 7.62mm mini-guns. The H model is similar, except no 7.62mm mini-guns and one of the 40mm guns is replaced with a 105mm Howitzer. Both models have advanced sensors and target acquisition system including forward-looking infrared radar (FLIR) and low-light TV. Weapons employment accuracy is outstanding. This aircraft is vulnerable to enemy air defense systems and must operate in a-low threat environment.

*Denotes aircraft with FM capability.

Air Operations

AIR ASSAULT

Successful air assault execution is based on a careful analysis of METT-T and detailed, precise reverse planning. Five basic plans that comprise the reverse planning sequence are developed for each air assault operation.

They are:

1. *Ground Tactical Plan.* The foundation of a successful air assault operation is the commander's ground tactical plan. All additional plans must support this plan. The plan specifies actions in the objective area to ultimately accomplish the mission and address subsequent operations.

2. *The Landing Plan.* The landing plan must support the ground tactical plan. This plan outlines a sequence of events that allows elements to move into the area of operations, and ensures that units arrive at designated locations at prescribed times prepared to execute the ground tactical plan.

3. *The Air Movement Plan.* The air movement plan is based on the ground tactical and landing plans. It specifies the schedule and provides instructions for air movement of troops, equipment, and supplies from pickup zones (PZs) to landing zones (LZs).

4. *The Loading Plan.* The loading plan is based on the air movement plan. It ensures that troops, equipment, and supplies are loaded on the correct aircraft. Unit integrity is maintained when aircraft loads are planned. Cross-loading

may be necessary in order to ensure survivability of command and control assets, and the mix of weapons systems arriving at the LZ.

5. *The Staging Plan.* The staging plan is based on the loading plan and prescribes the arrival time of ground units (troops, equipment and supplies) at the PZ in the order of movement

SELECTION AND MARKING OF PZS/LZS.

Small-unit leaders should consider the following when selecting a PZ/LZ:

1. *Size.* Minimal circular landing point separation from other aircraft and obstacles is needed:

   Observation helicopters—25 meters

   UH-1, AH-1—35 meters

   UH-60, AH-64—50 meters

   Cargo helicopters—80 meters

2. *Surface conditions.* Avoid potential hazards (e.g. sand, blowing dust, snow, tree stumps, large rocks).

3. *Ground slope.*

   0%–6 %—land upslope

   7%–15%—land sideslope

   Over 15%—no touchdown (aircraft may hover)

4. *Obstacles.* An obstacle clearance ratio of 10 to 1 is used in planning approach to and departure from the PZ and LZ (i.e. a ten foot tall tree requires 100 feet of horizontal distance for approach or departure). Obstacles will be marked with a red ChemLight at night or red panels during the daytime. Markings will not be used if they cause the position to be seen by the enemy.

5. *Approach/Departure.* Approach and departure are made into the wind and along the long axis of the PZ/LZ.

6. *Loads.* The greater the load, the larger the PZ/LZ must be to accommodate the insertion or extraction.

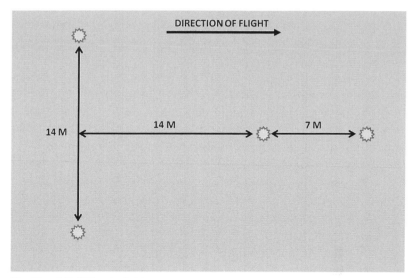

Marking LZs/PZs at night

MARKING PZS AND LZS.

Day. A ground guide will mark the PZ or LZ for the lead aircraft by holding an rifle over his head, by displaying a folded VS-17 panel chest high, or by other coordinated and identifiable means.

Night. The code letter Y (Inverted Y) is used to mark the landing point of the lead aircraft at night. Chemical lights or "beanbag" lights are used to maintain light discipline. A swinging Chem-Light(r) may also be used to mark the landing point.

PZ OPERATIONS

Prior to arrival of aircraft, the PZ is secured, the PZ control party is positioned, and the troops and equipment are positioned in platoon/squad assembly areas.

When the squad leader occupies the assembly area he ensures that security of the assembly area is being conducted, communications with the aircraft and the TCE are maintained, and his squad is formed and prepared to load the aircraft.

The use of aircraft in operations always carries an inherent risk. Soldiers should keep the following safety considerations in mind when operating around aircraft:

- Always approach the aircraft from 90 to 45 degrees off the nose.
- When on the aircraft, weapons loaded with live ammunition should be carried with the muzzles pointing down.
- Wear a ballistic helmet.
- When possible, an air crew safety brief for all personnel should be conducted, covering at a minimum loading and offloading, emergencies, and egress procedures.
- Leaders need to carry a manifest and turn a copy in to higher.

LOADING

Loading Using One Door. The tracker squad leader initiates movement once the aircraft has landed. The squad moves to the near side of the aircraft in a file formation. The tracker squad leader

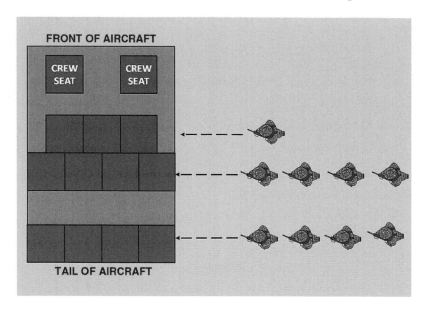

always leads the group and ensures all personnel and equipment are loaded and all squad members are buckled up in their assigned seats. The squad leader notifies the crew chief when all squad members are on board and ready for liftoff.

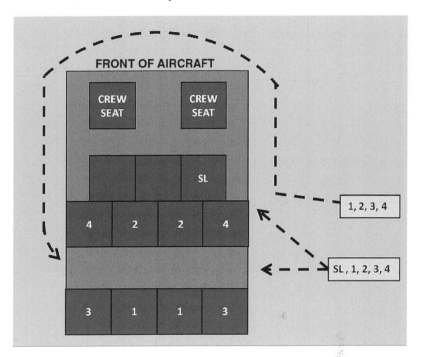

Loading Using Two Doors. The tracker squad leader initiates movement once the aircraft has landed. The far-side and near-side teams move to the aircraft in a file formation. The tracker squad leader always leads the near-side group and ensures all personnel and equipment are loaded and all squad members are buckled up in their assigned seats. The squad leader notifies the crew chief when all squad members are on board and ready for liftoff.

EXITING THE AIRCRAFT
The one-side off-load or the two-side off-load is used when exiting a rotary-wing aircraft with side doors. When the aircraft is config-

ured with a rear ramp the trackers will exit from the rear of the aircraft. The trackers must be careful to avoid the main and tail rotors of the aircraft while exiting as well as the rotors of other aircraft that have landed with them. The type of aircraft, the distance between aircraft, and the number of aircraft that can fit on the LZ at one time are critical considerations when determining which exiting technique to use.

One-Side Off-Load. The one-side off-load is the slowest of the off-loading techniques but simplifies command and control of the squad on the LZ. It also allows the door gunners on the opposite side of the aircraft to engage the enemy during off-loading.

Trackers exit from one side of the aircraft and take up a prone position, forming a 180-degree security perimeter on that side of the aircraft. The trackers should remain in the prone position until the aircraft lifts off before departing the LZ. The tracker squad

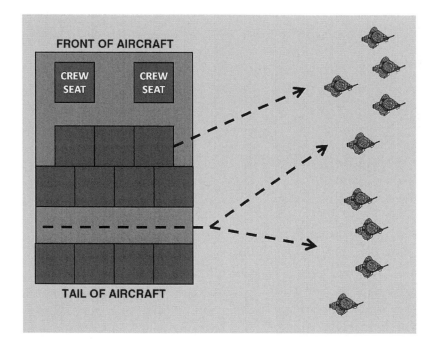

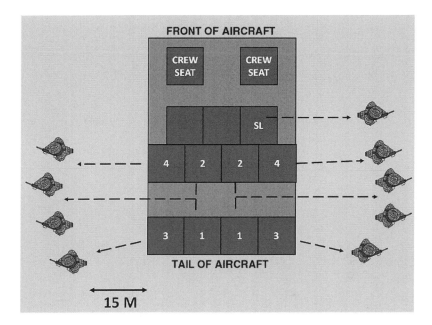

leader directs his squad to move directly to the nearest covered and concealed position.

Two-Side Off-Load. The two-side off-load is the quickest technique for exiting an aircraft.

Trackers exit from both sides of the aircraft and take up a prone position, forming a 180-degree security perimeter on each side of the aircraft. The trackers should remain in the prone position until the aircraft lifts off before departing the LZ. The tracker squad leader directs his squad to move directly to the nearest covered and concealed position.

Rear-Ramp Off-Load. The combat tracker squad exits from the rear ramp of the aircraft. The squad then moves out away from the aircraft and drops to a prone fighting position, establishing a 180-degree security perimeter to the rear of the aircraft until it departs the LZ. Once the aircraft departs the LZ, the tracker squad leader directs his squad to move directly to the nearest covered and concealed position.

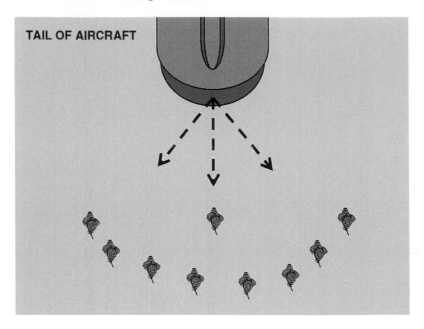

Support Request Quick Reference Guide

GRID MISSION—EXAMPLE

Observer	Firing Unit
F2W, this is S2A, ADJUST FIRE, OVER.	S2A, this is F2W, AJUST FIRE, OUT.
GRID WM180513, DIRECTION 0530, OVER.	GRID WM180513, DIRECTION 0530, OVER.
Armed insurgents in the open, OVER.	Armed insurgents in the open, OUT.
	SHOT OVER.
SHOT OUT.	SPLASH OVER
SPLASH OUT	
End of mission, 15 casualties, OVER	End of mission, 15 casualties, OUT.

SHIFT FROM KNOWN POINT—EXAMPLE

Observer	Firing Unit
F2W, this is S2A, ADJUST	F2W, this is F24, ADJUST
FIRE, SHIFT AB1201, OUT.	FIRE, SHIFT AB1201, OUT.
DIRECTION 2420, RIGHT 400, ADD 400, OUT.	DIRECTION 2420, RIGHT 400, ADD 400, OUT.
5 insurgent trucks in the open, OVER	5 insurgent trucks in the open, AUTHENTICATE Juliet OVER
I AUTHENTICATE Tango OVER	ROGER, SHOT OVER.
SHOT OUT	SPLASH, OVER.
SPLASH OUT.	
End of mission, 5 trucks destroyed, OVER.	End of mission, 5 trucks destroyed, OUT.

FIVE-LINE EMERGENCY CLOSE AIR SUPPORT REQUEST

Contact Frequency: _____

Call Sign: _____

1. Check In/Situation: _____

Friendly Mark: _____
(Don't give your position grid unless absolutely necessary.)

"(Assasin19) this is (S2W). My team has just been ambushed on route "RED" about 20 kilometers north of CP "Arizona" we are taking overwhelming effective fire. Friendly position is marked with purple smoke. I am an untrained controller requesting emergency close air support."

2. Target Location: _____

Target Elevation:_____
or
Target Direction/Distance: _____ /_____ **meters**

"From my position, the enemy is north 200 meters on the south side of the mountain overlooking the river. Elevation is approximately 4000 ft." (give elevation, if possible)

3. Target Description:_____

Target Marking: _____

"There are dismounted enemy to the north across the river firing at us from behind cover. I am marking their position with tracer fire."

4. Threats: _____

Restrictions: _____

"There are no immediate threats to you; do not engage anything south of the river."

5. Remarks/Effects Requested: _____

"Be advised I have friendlies located 100 meters west of my position on the south side of the river; request immediate suppression of enemy positions."

NOTES
- Announce "I am an untrained controller" on check-in.
- Speak slowly in plain English; avoid acronyms and abbreviations.
- Be 100 percent sure you and the aircrew are talking about the same thing; ask what he sees

NINE-LINE MEDEVAC REQUEST

Line #1: 6-digit grid coordinate of the pick-up site.

Line #2: Radio frequency, call sign, and suffix of the requesting unit.

Line #3: Number of patients by precedence.
1. The purpose of classifying patients by precedence is so that the medevac element can establish a priority as to which patients are to be evacuated first. Normally, time is a factor, which determines the categories of precedence.
2. There are four priorities of precedence:
   - **Urgent:** Is assigned to emergency cases that should be evacuated as soon as possible and within a maximum of 2 hours to save life, limb, or eyesight, to prevent complication of serious illness, or to avoid permanent disability.
   - **Urgent-Surgical:** Is assigned to patients who must receive far forward surgical intervention to save life and stabilize for permanent evacuation.

- **Priority:** Is assigned to sick and wounded personnel requiring prompt medical care. This precedence is used when the individual should be evacuated within four hours or his condition could deteriorate to such a degree that he will become an Urgent precedence, or whose requirements for special treatment are not readily available locally, or who will suffer unnecessary pain or disability.
- **Routine:** Is assigned to sick and wounded personnel requiring evacuation but whose condition is not expected to deteriorate significantly. The sick and wounded in this category should be evacuated within 24 hours.
- **Convenience:** Is assigned to patients for whom evacuation by medical vehicle is a matter of medical convenience rather than necessity.

Line #4: Special equipment needed:
1. Aircraft Rescue Hoist: Utilized on both the UH1V and UH-60A. The cable is 256 feet long with 250 feet of usable cable, with a tensile strength of 600 pounds. The hoist has two settings, a fast and a slow setting; the fast setting can lift 300 pounds at 250 feet per minute, the slow setting can lift 600 pounds at 125 feet per minute.
2. Jungle/Forest Penetrator: Used on the rescue hoist for casualty extraction from dense forest or jungle. The penetrator is limited to three (3) casualties or 600 pounds. The jungle/forest penetrator weighs 21 ½ lb., is 34 in. long and 8 in. in diameter. The three legs are 11 ½ in. long and 4 ¾ in. wide.
3. Semi-Rigid Litter: Used for casualties with other than back injuries. Limited to one (1) casualty or 400 pounds.
4. Stokes Basic Litter: Used for casualties with injuries, including neck and back injuries, that require immobilization.

5. Kendrick Extrication Device (KED): Semi-rigid support used to immobilize casualties with minor neck and back injuries, same limitations as the Stokes basic litter.

Line #5: Number of patients by type:
1. Litter patients.
2. Ambulatory patients.

Line #6: Situation.
1. Wartime Situation:
   - No enemy troops in the area.
   - Possible enemy troops in the area.
   - Enemy in the area, approach with caution.
   - Enemy troops in the area, armed escort required.
2. Peacetime Situation:
   - Gunshot, shrapnel.
   - Broken bones.
   - Illness.

Line #7: Method of marking the site.

Line #8: Patient nationality and status.
1. U.S. Military.
2. U.S. Civilian.
3. Non-U.S. Military.
4. Non-U.S. Civilian.
5. Prisoner of War.

Line #9:
1. NBC contamination (if applicable)—RADS/Hour or type agent used, if known, in the area of the pick-up site.
2. Description of the terrain in and around the pick-up site to aid the pilot in locating your site.

The Combat Tracker's Load

Mobility is key for a combat tracker to successfully perform his mission and survive on the battlefield. The combat tracker squad needs to travel as light as possible if they are to close the time and distance gap between them and their quarry. The combat tracker's load is the mission-essential equipment required for the combat tracker to fight and survive during that operation. The tracker cannot be expected to carry gear for every possible contingency or combat situation. Instead, his load must be based on his particular mission and the ability to remain mobile.

The tracker's ability to react to the enemy is reduced when he is burdened with a heavy load. Heavy loads cause physical and mental fatigue and can place trackers in mortal danger if they have to rapidly react to enemy contact. Fighting loads must be light so that tracker can remain alert, agile, and stealthy. The squad leader, through the conduct of pre-combat inspections, will ensure his tracker squad has all the mission-essential equipment required to carry out their mission.

Equipment is broken down into several categories:

- **Level 1:** Describes the uniform and equipment that is worn by the individual tracker. These items are the uniform, boots, belt, dog tags, and any items carried on his person.
- **Level 2:** Describes the fighting load carried by the tracker. These items are typically the tracker's individual weapon,

basic load of ammunition, load-bearing equipment, and helmet (if worn). The fighting load should not exceed 48 pounds.

- **Level 3:** Describes the approach march load carried for extended operations. The tracker must carry enough equipment and munitions for longer operations until resupply. The approach march load (which includes the fighting load) should be less than 72 pounds.

- **Special Equipment:** Describes the equipment that is mission-specific.

The following pages give an example of the type of equipment a tracker might carry on a pursuit operation. Understand that every mission is different and the equipment carried will depend on the mission, enemy situation, terrain, and weather, as well as the expected duration of the mission.

LEVEL 1

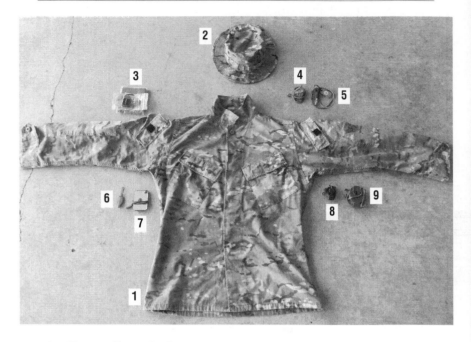

1. **Camouflage Jacket.** Jacket should be loose fitting and untailored, with plenty of room in pockets to carry mission-essential items. Each arm has a 1-inch-square piece of infrared identification, friend or foe (IFF) tape attached.
2. **Camouflage Headgear.** Headgear (patrol cap, boonie hat, or watch cap) will depend on the mission and climate. A 1-inch piece of infrared IFF tape can be placed on the top of the headgear for identification by friendly air.
3. **Signal Device.** Phoenix IR-15 programmable transmitter with a 9-volt battery for covertly marking one's position at night,

and a 10-by-10-inch orange signal square cut from a VS-17 Panel. This panel is used as a recognition signal device for linking up with other ground elements.

4. **Identification Tags.** These provide the soldier's basic information for casualty identification.

5. **SAR Eclipse Signal Device.** The SAR Eclipse is a "Back to Basics—No Batteries Required" piece of signal/survival equipment. It is constructed from two US Geological Survey rust-resistant, high-grade stainless steel identification tags. One tag has a dull matt finish with a piece of SOLAS 3M high-intensity reflective tape for night signaling. The other tag has a near mirror polish for daytime signaling. This device, although very compact, has been observed in tests out to 10 miles during daylight conditions and out to 250 meters at night using a standard Mag-Lite flashlight.

6. **INOVA Microlight.** This small flashlight comes in white, green, blue, and red and is perfect for signaling or conducting map checks at night.

7. **Signal Mirror.** Besides its uses for signaling, applying camouflage, and shaving, a small mirror is also a good piece of equipment for deflecting and manipulating light in order to view details of an impression.

8. **Whistle.** A whistle comes in handy when having to signal commands to other friendly elements over gunfire.

9. **Magnetic Compass.** The tracker squad always needs to know where they are in relation to other friendly or enemy elements; they also need to be able to provide the general direction the enemy is moving. Although a GPS is a good piece of equipment it will never take the place of good compass.

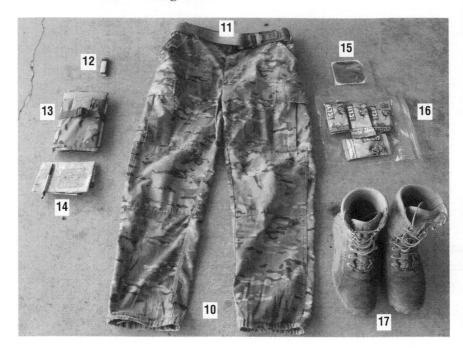

10. **Camouflage Trousers.** Trousers should be loose fitting and untailored, with plenty of room in pockets to carry mission-essential items. Tight-fitting clothing tears easier, allowing mosquitoes and other insects access to exposed areas.

11. **Rigger's Belt.**
12. **Lighter.**
13. **Notebook.** The notebook is used to record information gained during the mission; it also holds footprint data cards.
14. **Map, Protractor, and Pencil.** A tracker must always know where he and other friendly units are, and be able to conduct a map analysis to determine where the quarry may be going.
15. **Field-Expedient Patch Kit.** To quickly repair minor rips or tears in the uniform during a mission.
16. **Rations.** These should be high-energy food items that can be consumed quickly on the go without breaking into the rucksack.
17. **Boots.** Footwear depends on the environment the operation is being conducted in. All the members of the tracker squad should, however, attempt to wear boots with soles that have the same tread pattern. This way the squad will be able to distinguish their own footprint impressions from others.

LEVEL 2

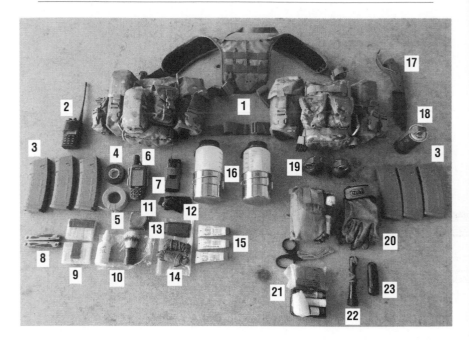

1. **Load-bearing Equipment (LBE).** This piece of equipment should be capable of carrying the minimum equipment necessary to fight and survive on the battlefield. It should be modular, so that it can be configured to meet the requirements of the mission, and comfortable to wear for prolonged periods.
2. **Radio.** The radio is probably the most important piece of equipment carried on the operation. It is the squad's lifeline for sending and receiving vital information to and from the TCE and for coordinating with other support assets. It should be lightweight and capable of communicating with air and ground assets when support is required.
3. **Magazines.** No more than a basic combat load of ammunition for the weapon system should be carried (i.e. 210 rounds for the M4) on the LBE.
4. **Electrical Tape.** To secure items together while in the field.

5. **Colored Surveyor's Tape.** For marking the last known sign.
6. **GPS.** The GPS is a good piece of equipment that can track the route of the squad and give the squad's precise location. However, do not become over-reliant on technology that is battery operated. When not pinpointing your location, keep the GPS turned off to conserve the battery life.
7. **Strobe Light with IR Cover.** For signaling friendly forces.
8. **Multi-tool.** Multi-tools are great for making small repairs and typically have a knife, a file, flat-tip and Philips-head screw drivers, a can opener, and pliers.
9. **Spare Batteries.** Enough for all equipment for the operation. When acquiring equipment, choose items that use the same type of batteries. AA batteries are compact, and common enough that they can be found just about anywhere in the world.
10. **Weapon Oil and Brush.** A bottle of oil to protect and lubricate your equipment is essential in any environment. A shaving brush can be used to brush dust and debris from equipment.
11. **Measuring Device.** For taking measurements of impressions or showing scale when taking pictures
12. **Headlamp.** A headlamp is a good item to have when it is important to have both hands free—for instance, when conducting a prisoner search or some type of exploitation.
13. **Knife Sharpener.** Carrying a sharpener is essential—your knife will be of no use if it is not sharp.
14. **550 Cord.** Twenty-five to thirty feet of cordage should be carried for repairing, tying, or lashing items.
15. **Camouflage Face Cream.** Camouflaging exposed skin will help the tracker blend into the natural environment and prevent him from compromising the squad's position.
16. **Water Bottles.** At least two quarts of water should be carried. The basic wide-mouthed 32 oz Nalgene bottles are best for any environment. Steel cups should be carried as well for cooking or heating up liquids.

17. **Knife.** A multipurpose knife that has at least a six-inch blade should be carried. The knife should be heavy, sharp, and versatile enough to be used for building shelter and survival tasks as well as in fighting. This knife pictured on page 246 was a collaborative design between the author and custom knife maker Jeff Crowner.

18. **Smoke Grenade.** At least one HC smoke grenade should be carried for screening or signaling.

19. **Fragmentation Grenades.** At least two fragmentation grenades should be carried when on patrol.

20. **Gloves.** Should be used to camouflage hands and protect them from sharp objects. Gloves with a reinforced palm are typically best.

21. **Individual First Aid Kit.** This kit provides the necessary equipment to perform first aid on oneself or another squad member, and should address the two leading causes of death on the battlefield, severe hemorrhage and inadequate airway. The kit should include: tourniquet, 2 elastic bandages, a 4½" gauze bandage, adhesive surgical tape, airway nasopharyngeal, 4 exam gloves, 2 PriMed gauze bandages, EMS shears, triangular bandage, and water purification tablets.

22. **Mag-Lite Flashlight.** For tracking at night.

23. **Blast Match.** A Blast Match is another great fire-producing survival tool designed for all-weather use; it can be operated with one hand in case of injury. Even in the most wet environments this device will still be capable of starting a fire.

Rifle. The rifle is what is issued. Contrary to popular belief, soldiers and law enforcement officers don't get to pick and choose their weapon systems nor the caliber they shoot. Regardless of the type of weapon issued, the operator needs to be an expert with the assigned weapon. The tracker needs to be proficient on how to employ the weapon, knowing its capabilities and limitations and how to perform maintenance and small repairs—as well as being an expert marksman with it.

Weapon Accessories. Optical scopes or red dot sights may be required for the mission depending on METT-T. A target pointer, illuminator, or aiming light is good to have for operations at night.

LEVEL 3

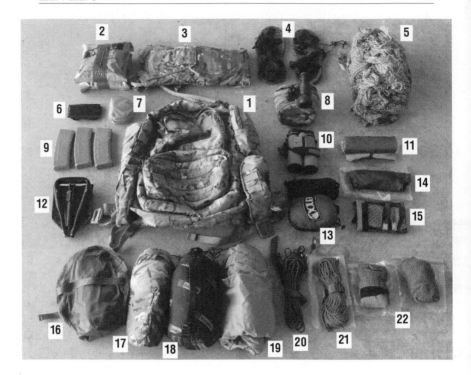

1. **Rucksack.** This piece of equipment holds all mission-essential equipment that is to be carried by the tracker for extended operations. The size of this pack is dictated by the amount of equipment the tracker will need to sustain himself till a resupply can be requested. The estimated time on operation, terrain, and weather conditions will all be factors to be considered.
2. **Rations.** Enough rations for forty-eight to seventy-two hours should be carried.
3. **Three-liter Hydration System.** The tracker will need to carry enough water to last until the end of the operation, or until a suitable water source is found or resupply occurs. Water is always consumed from the pack first. Should the pack be dropped for any reason during the operation the tracker should have full canteens on the LBE.

4. **Carlton's CAT PAWS (Super Sneakers).** CAT PAWS are a great item to place over the soles of the boot to conceal the tracker's own tracks.
5. **Viper Hood.** The Viper hood breaks up the recognizable and familiar shape of the human head and shoulders. The best aspect of the Viper is that it is designed to be worn in conjunction with the tracker's combat equipment, without interfering with the tracker's ability to get to the pouches on the LBE.
6. **Large Trash Bag.** For waterproofing or for storing trash while on operation.
7. **Weapons Cleaning Kit.** This kit should be capable of maintaining the weapon in a field environment. At a minimum the kit should contain a bore brush, chamber brush, cleaning rod, slotted tip for patches, patches, CLP, lens brush for optics, and all-purpose utility brush.
8. **Night-vision Device.** Night vision is necessary when conducting operations at night.
9. **Spare Magazines.** Three extra loaded magazines.
10. **Binoculars.** Should be used whenever possible to detect the enemy from a distance. Binoculars provide a larger field of view than a monocular or scope.
11. **VS-17 Panel.** The VS17 Signal Panel can be laid out on the ground to identify troop positions to friendly aircraft, or to identify where help is needed.
12. **E- Tool.** The e-tool is a lightweight collapsible shovel that can be used for digging or chopping.
13. **Hammock.** Depending on the operational environment, a hammock may be essential for staying dry when bedding down for the night.
14. **Sewing and Equipment Repair Kit.** This should include sewing thread, needles, and safety pins.
15. **Hygiene Kit.** Minimal hygiene items such as nail clippers, toothbrush and toothpaste, and a small washrag.
16. **Compression Sack or Waterproof Bag.**

17. **Basha/Tarp.** This needs to be large enough to be used as a makeshift litter to transport a casualty and to provide protection from the elements if as a shelter.

18. **Sleeping Gear.** Depending on the environment, this could range from a sleeping system and a ground mat for extreme temperatures to a poncho liner for more tropical climates.

19. **Gortex Bivy.** This bivy provides a waterproof, breathable cover that keeps out wind, snow, and rain.

20. **Bungee Cords.** For quick lashing of items such as the tarp.

21. **550 Cord.** The tracker should carry a another twenty-five to thirty feet of cordage in the rucksack in addition to the cordage he carries on his person.

22. **Spare Socks.** Foot maintenance is imperative. Dry, clean socks will help prevent blisters, hotspots, and athlete's foot.

SPECIAL EQUIPMENT

1. **Digital Camera.** A great piece of equipment for recording evidence to be used in the tracker's debrief or to be circulated further to other elements involved in the pursuit.
2. **POGO Printer.** This piece of equipment can potentially save time when recording impressions. This device, when connected to a digital camera, can print a digital picture of the quarry's footprint impression to be circulated among the trackers. The Polaroid sheets it prints onto have an adhesive backing that allow them to be stuck directly onto a footprint ID card.

Glossary

As in many other types of work, trackers use special terms to communicate to each other and their commanders. Following are common terms trackers need to know if they are to communicate with each other effectively.

Activity Indicators. Footprints or other marks left on the ground that indicate that a certain identifiable action took place.

Backtrack. To track back to the area from which the quarry came.

Cold Track. Track that is more than one day old.

Combat Tracker Team (CTT). Four-man section of trained visual trackers within a combat tracker squad; it consists of a tracker, two flank security team members, and a team leader.

Combat Tracking. Aggressive tracking techniques employed by a trained tracking team during combat conditions; designed to rapidly establish or reestablish contact with the enemy, collect information about the enemy, or rescue lost or missing friendly personnel.

Combat Tracking Operation. Mission conducted by one or more combat tracker squads to gather intelligence or aggressively pursue and establish contact with the enemy.

Combat Tracking Squad (CTS). Nine-man unit trained in visual tracking techniques; the smallest military unit capable of providing its own security and conducting fire and maneuver. The combat tracker squad contains two four-man tracker teams and a squad leader. The squad leader has two subordinate team leaders who lead their respective combat tracker teams.

Conclusive Sign. Sign that can be positively connected to or associated with the quarry.

Contamination. Sign unrelated to the quarry that obscures the quarry's sign. Contamination occurs when a track line enters an area where numerous other tracks exist or when other humans, animals, or vehicles enter the area of the track line.

Countertracking Techniques. Attempts by the quarry to conceal tracks or lose, delay, or cause harm to his pursuers.

Cutting for Sign. Searching for sign in order to establish a starting point from which to begin tracking.

Entry Point/Exit Point. Points where the quarry entered or exited an incident site.

Flank Security (FS). Team members (a minimum of two) whose primary responsibility is to prevent the tracker and team leader from being ambushed.

Gait. The specific manner in which a person walks, runs, or moves on foot. The ability to identify the quarry's gait will assist the tracker in identifying the quarry's track picture.

Hot Debrief. Immediate debrief upon returning from a patrol in order to pass on time-sensitive information.

Hot Track. Track that is no more than two hours old.

Incident Site. The site where an event or action occurred that is linked to the quarry.

Inconclusive Sign. Sign that cannot be confirmed as belonging to the quarry but, with other evidence taken into account, is likely to have been made by him.

Initial Start Point (ISP). The point on the ground where a tracker squad begins following sign made by the quarry. It may or may not be the incident site.

Inventing Sign. When the tracker convinces himself that he sees the quarry's sign when in reality none exists.

Key Print. A footprint impression that stands out.

Last Known Sign (LKS). Last sign the tracker can positively identify as the quarry's.

Lost Track Drill (LTD). Systematic techniques performed to acquire or reacquire the track line; starts with an individual drill conducted by the tracker and escalates into larger drills that include other members of the lead tracker team.

Medium. Environment in which sign or evidence was made.

Natural State. State of the environment unaffected by sign.

Opening. Passageway in vegetation the quarry may have moved through.

Patrol Debrief. Report generated to record all information gained from an operation.

Pointers. Sign that indicates the direction of movement, such as trampled grass pushed forward.

Probe. To move from the last known sign forward to search for additional sign.

Pursue. Attempt to establish or reestablish contact with the quarry in order to capture or kill him.

Quarry. Person or persons being pursued.

Sign. General term used to describe any indicator created by the quarry's passage.

Squad Leader (SL). Member of the squad responsible for everything the squad does or fails to do, including all training and tactical decisions as well as the health and welfare of the entire squad.

Step-by-step Tracking. Systematic technique that teaches a tracker to detect sign made by each step taken in sequence.

Team Leader (TL). Member of the tracker team responsible for everything his team does or fails to do, including all training and tactical decisions as well as the health and welfare of the team.

Time-Distance Gap. Theoretical time and distance the quarry is in front of the squad tracking him; it is based on the age of the sign and the time passed since the incident took place.

Track Line. Continuous line of observable sign left by the quarry.

Track Picture. Interpretation of the quarry's activities based on all evidence observed.

Track Separation Point (TSP). Point on the ground where the sign splits into two or more different directions, indicating that the quarry separated into two or more groups.

Track Trap. Natural or man-made area that captures impressions made by the quarry's passage.

Tracking. Capability of following and interpreting a trail of sign made by the quarry.

Tracker (TR). Member of a tracker team who looks for, interprets, and follows sign.

Tracker Control Element (TCE). The command and control (C2) element responsible for the employment of multiple tracker units; it supports the teams by tracking their movements on a situation map and collecting and disseminating information to ensure that the units are properly supported. The TCE may be co-located at a stationary tactical operations center (TOC) or employed as a mobile tracker control element.

Tracker Support Group (TSG). Maneuver element that provides direct support should the combat tracker squad become engaged with its enemy. This "finishing force" is typically an infantry platoon.

Trail. To follow the quarry while staying out of his sight; usually used to gather information about the quarry or his movements.

Warm Track. Track that is more than two hours old but no more than one day old.

About The Author

John Hurth is a retired U.S. Army Special Forces soldier who served with the 1st Special Forces Group at Ft. Lewis, Washington, where he participated in multiple deployments overseas, including two combat tours in support of the Global War On Terror. John also served with the Special Operations Training Detachment at the Joint Readiness Training Center (JRTC) in Ft. Polk, Louisiana, coaching, teaching, and mentoring Special Operations units undergoing training at JRTC. Prior to joining the Special Forces he served as an infantry soldier in multiple airborne, light, and mechanized infantry assignments within the continental U.S. and overseas.

John was first introduced to tracking by a Vietnam veteran noncommissioned officer, who taught him to recognize and follow sign. John continued to refine his tracking capabilities throughout his military service during both peacetime and wartime.

After retiring, John put his years of tracking knowledge and experience to use working as the program lead and head instructor for the U.S. Army's Combat Tracker Course at Ft. Huachuca, Arizona. He managed and oversaw the conduct and resourcing of the Army's Combat Tracker Course and instructed many U.S. and foreign military students in combat tracker techniques. John is now the president and chief tracking instructor at TÝR Group LLC, based in Louisiana.

Index

259